Organising Industrial Activities Across Firm Boundaries

The way in which industrial activities are organised among firms has been a fundamental theoretical concern for a long time. In practice firms have found these matters, referred to as make-or-buy issues, difficult to analyse. This book investigates how industrial activity can be organised efficiently when the work is divided between different firms.

Organising Industrial Activities Across Firm Boundaries provides an overview of the theoretical background to these issues before developing an original analysis based upon an activity based framework. The classical problem of vertical integration is dealt with as a matter of how to analyse and obtain efficiency in activity structures involving several participants. These issues are examined in a major case study with four embedded cases addressing various aspects of the activity structures. The book also provides a detailed analysis of the interdependence, boundaries and dynamics of activity structures.

The make-or-buy issue is central to both economics and business administration with applications for production, purchasing and marketing issues. *Organising Industrial Activities Across Firm Boundaries* is an original and stimulating analysis of this important area.

ROUTLEDGE STUDIES IN BUSINESS
ORGANISATION AND NETWORKS

Organising Industrial Activities Across Firm Boundaries

Anna Dubois

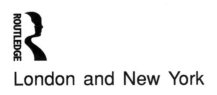

London and New York

First published 1998
by Routledge
11 New Fetter Lane, London EC4P 4EE

Simultaneously published in the USA and Canada
by Routledge
29 West 35th Street, New York, NY 10001

Typeset in Times by Florencetype Ltd, Stoodleigh, Devon.
Printed and bound in Great Britain by Antony Rowe Ltd.,
Chippenham, Wiltshire

British Library Cataloguing in Publication Data
A catalogue record for this book is available from the British Library

Library of Congress Cataloguing in Publication Data
A catalogue record for this book has been requested

ISBN 0-415-14707-7

Contents

List of figures and tables

FIGURES

TABLES

Preface

This book deals with activities. In order to perform activities resources are needed. The thinking, data collecting and writing activities that resulted in this book required many resources, only a small part of which were my own.

Intellectual resources were provided by three men. Lars-Erik Gadde generously contributed to the thinking activities by letting me share his analytical resources. Fortunately, he also turned out to have inexhaustible resources of patience. Håkan Håkansson was not very patient and thereby a perfect complement to Lars-Erik. G.B. Richardson, whom I never met, contributed his brilliant article, without which I would not have found my way through the thinking.

The thinking and writing activities were also improved and made more joyful by cheerful comments and encouragement from my colleagues at Chalmers: Lennart Bångens, Ragnar Hörndahl, Oskar Jellbo, Jonna Sandell, Daniel Olsson, Kajsa Hulthén and Barbro Strömberg. In addition, Mia Eriksson, Yimane Ketema, Anna Reuithe, Ivan Snehota, Torkel Wedin, Alexandra Waluszewski and Maria Åsberg at Uppsala University, and Åge Garnes, Jan-Frode Jansson, Ann-Charlott Pedersen and Tim Torvatn at The Norwegian Institute of Technology contributed comments and fruitful disputes.

Springtime in Lancaster must also be considered a resource. Geoff Easton, Luis Araujo and Christina Georgeieva at Lancaster University helped me to make it productive.

The data collecting activities required empirical resources. These were generously provided, especially by the purchasing department at the case company. Kent, Stig, Sven-Olof and Manne not only gave me all the information I asked for, they also made the data collection a real pleasure.

In the end, an anonymous referee contributed inspiring comments and advice which made me extend the thinking and writing a little further.

To complete the writing activities, extensive language expertise was required. Linda Schenck provided invaluable support in correcting the final manuscript. Christine Räisänen helped me with earlier drafts and paper writings, constantly asking: *What is this?* – which indeed was, and still is, a highly relevant question.

Many thanks to all of you!

Anna Dubois
March, 1997

Acknowledgements

The research programme of which the project underlying this book was a part was mainly sponsored by Axel och Margaret Ax:son Johnsons Stiftelse för allmännyttiga ändamål. Financial support was also provided by Torsten och Ragnar Söderbergs Stiftelser and The Swedish National Board of Technology and Industry.

The data collection with regard to the hydraulic system case presented in Chapter 3 was jointly carried out with Jan-Frode Jansson at The Norwegian Institute of Technology.

A previous version of the machine body case presented in Chapter 3 also appears in Håkansson, H. and Snehota, I. (1995) *Developing Relationships in Business Networks*, London: Routledge.

Chapter 1

Introduction

During the development of a new truck model, SweFork – a manufacturer of electrical trucks for materials handling – had to decide what parts of the new truck should be produced in-house and what parts should be bought from suppliers. Numerous aspects had to be considered and during the development process additional aspects arose which made the situation complex and difficult to overview. In addition, when the production of the new truck begun, various changes in design and production had to be effected, which altered the conditions for the decisions regarding whether to make or to buy the parts. Some of the considerations regarded as important for the make-or-buy decisions were related to SweFork's internal operations, while others were related to what the suppliers could do for them. One important internal aspect was that SweFork's own production capacity, used to produce several truck models, was under pressure, which favoured buying of the parts. Later, a decrease in demand for the trucks changed this situation, which became characterised by excess capacity. Moreover, numerous design changes, considered teething troubles, were needed during the first years of production, making it more difficult to buy than to make certain parts. This was a result of the fact that once a particular component had to be redesigned this often called for changes of related components which, in turn, entailed changes of components connected to them, and so forth. Consequently, these matters were complex to handle. This made it difficult to involve the various suppliers in the complicated problem solving process. As a result, the suppliers were often asked for quotations when the design of the components was already completed. Based on SweFork's drawings they then had to consider whether the components fitted into their current production operations and what adjustments were needed to cope with SweFork's requirements. For the suppliers, these considerations depended on how the operations needed to produce SweFork's components fitted those already undertaken by them for other customers. Hence, the suppliers' current production operations entailed both restraints and possibilities of various kinds. Some suppliers would have preferred to be involved in the design of the components since this would have made it possible for them to better relate the production activities for the new truck model with their existing ones.

The main question for SweFork may be seen as a practical one. Under what conditions would it be advantageous to let suppliers take on the production of individual parts of the truck? SweFork spent a great deal of time and effort in solving the make-or-buy problems. This resulted in certain cases in out-sourcing some part of the production, and in some cases in maintaining in-house production. However, no obvious solutions could be found as every make-or-buy situation was found to be closely connected with various other aspects. How to organise the activities within the firm turned out to be related to how these were connected with the suppliers' activities, and this is, in turn, was associated with how the suppliers related their activities to their suppliers and other customers, and so on. Thus, a more relevant articulation of the original question turned out to be how could the complex interrelations among all the parts and the activities needed to produce them be handled?

This book is an attempt to analyse situations of this kind. The issue is obviously important for firms handling make-or-buy situations in real life for their own good, as reflected in the example above. As early as in the 1940s Culliton pointed to the need for practical guidance in these matters and the need appears to remain.

> The most that is done is to list the possible advantages and disadvantages of making and of buying, without attempting to set up a satisfactory procedure for discovering whether, in a specific instance, making or buying could be expected to bring the greater advantages.
>
> (Culliton 1942: 1)

Although this may seem to be a rather practical problem, the issue is, and always has been, fundamental to the understanding of economic efficiency in industrial systems. Economists addressing the division of labour have attempted to design models explaining firm and industrial performance. However, to be able to generalise and aggregate the analysis they have simplified the context in which these problems are dealt with. Most often these simplifications encompass assumptions about independent firms and markets on which the firms exchange their products. These 'pure' forms of activity co-ordination, i.e., either through internal co-ordination (firm) of interdependent activities, or through market exchange of independent activities, seem, however, to be the exceptions rather than the rule in the real world. Interdependence of different kinds blurs the firm boundaries and thus makes individual make-or-buy situations difficult to delimit. The problems experienced by SweFork described above reflect some of the difficulties in every attempt to draw boundaries around firms and the things they do.

Table 1.1   Integration levels in the European automotive industry

Auto manufacturer	A	B	C	D	E	F	G	H	I	J
Added value by assembler	36	60	55	40	40	50	40	33	40	30
Bought from wholly owned subsidiaries	15	0	5	15	25	1	5	10	0	0
Level of integration (%)	51	60	60	55	65	51	45	43	40	30

Source: Lamming 1989

Dealing with interdependence among activities in industrial systems, this book provides a framework for analysis of the make-or-buy problems experienced by firms, as well as the theoretical issue of the industrial division of labour.

In the remainder of this chapter a further presentation of the practical and theoretical background to the problem is presented. Chapter 2 provides a framework for analysis of the efficiency of activity structures in industrial systems. Chapter 3 provides empirical illustrations of the complexity characterising activity structures and how the interdependence among activities causes problems when changes are effectuated. In Chapter 4 the activity interdependence is further analysed and in Chapter 5 certain boundaries resulting from the interdependence are identified. Lastly, in Chapter 6 some questions related to the dynamics of industrial systems are raised.

PRACTICAL BACKGROUND

Empirical studies have shown that the degree of vertical integration differs extensively among firms even in one and the same industry. Lamming's (1989) study, carried out within the European automotive industry, identified degrees of vertical integration varying between 30 and 65 per cent (see Table 1.1).

The large variation in the degree of vertical integration even within industries is interesting, as it implies that there are no given rules or answers as to how much should be made in-house and how much should be bought from suppliers. In addition, differences in terms of the degree of vertical integration among firms in different countries have also been found (Ford *et al.* 1993; see Table 1.2).

A study of 123 Swedish firms showed that 70 per cent of them purchased more than 40 per cent of their turnover and, for almost every fifth firm, that the purchase share extended 70 per cent (Håkansson 1989). Thus, large variations in vertical integration in industries as well as between countries have been identified. There are no clear reasons for this variation.

Table 1.2   Purchases as a percentage of sales in four countries

		UK	Canada	US	Australia
Purchases as a percentage of sales	< 30%	23	24	17	12
	30–49%	20	29	44	37
	50–59%	16	4	11	9
	> 60%	30	–	–	9

Source: Ford *et al.* 1993

However, there is evidence of decreasing degrees of vertical integration in general. According to Ford *et al.* (1993: 208): 'There appears to be some consensus that there is an increasing move towards "buy" rather than "make" and that this is a good idea'.

Their empirical survey, including UK, US, Canadian and Australian firms, supported this tendency of firms moving towards increasing their purchase rate, although some firms moved in the opposite direction. The tendency towards decreasing degrees of vertical integration has also been identified by others (Dirrheimer and Hubner 1983; Barreyre 1988; Lamming 1993). According to Barreyre out-sourcing, or 'impartition' as he calls it, is not a new phenomenon since, for instance, subcontracting was common centuries ago in areas such as shipbuilding and textile industries (Barreyre 1988: 509). However, historically the general behaviour was to make rather than to buy:

> Sixty years ago large manufacturing companies in Europe as well as in the USA had a strong propensity to vertical integration. For several reasons the fully integrated factory of Henry Ford was a model for many firms. Managers were often reluctant to sub-contract, for instance; they tended to minimise external dependency, freight or taxes in order to get a better added value/sales ratio. Although exceptions could be mentioned, this pattern of behaviour prevailed for years in the pre-marketing era and the heritage has not yet entirely disappeared. Consequently, until the end of the 1960s, nations primarily exchanged either raw materials or fully finished products; international production-sharing was little developed compared to what it is at present.
>
> (Barreyre 1988: 518)

Furthermore, Barreyre (1988: 510) goes on to argue that both the importance and the frequency of out-sourcing decisions are increasing, which he explains in terms of six major attributes or changes in the environment:

1 Accelerating technological change and obsolescence, which require faster depreciation of capital and know-how investments.
2 Discontinuity, which accentuates the need for organisational flexibility in the short term and strategic mobility in the long run.

3 The difficulty of maintaining sufficient company profitability in a context of crisis.
4 The increasing complexity of many products and the variety of processes necessary to produce each part of the whole.
5 The growing number of laws, rules and regulations which impose social constraints on firms in advanced societies and which accentuate the rigidity of industrial systems.
6 The intense world-wide competition which is both a cause and a consequence of striving for increased productivity through large-scale production.

The first and fourth points, dealing with technological change resulting in increasing technological complexity of both products and production processes, have been especially emphasised by others (Hayes and Abernathy 1980; Ford et al. 1993; Gadde and Håkansson 1993). Ford et al. (1993: 213) argue that 'no company possesses all of the technologies that are the basis of the design, manufacture and marketing of their offerings'. For this reason, firms are dependent upon the skills of others: 'Increasingly, the escalating costs of R&D, the rate of technological change, and the "intensity" of the technology in many products means that this dependence on others is growing' (Ford et al. 1993: 213).

Thus, the general tendency seems to be towards buying rather than making. However, regardless of the direction of make-or-buy decisions, they also seem to be problematic for the firms undertaking them for several reasons. In addition, they seem to be neglected as strategic issues (Culliton 1942; Jauch and Wilson 1972; Leenders and Nollet 1984; Ford et al. 1993). As early as in 1942 Culliton argued that firms often disregarded the presence and importance of these considerations: 'It is not improbable ... that some of the businessmen who said that they had no make or buy problems, more accurately could be said to have had the problems but failed to recognise them' (Culliton 1942: 2).

More recently, Ford et al. (1993) found evidence of the problem still existing arguing that: '... few companies takes a strategic view of which of their supposedly mainstream activities could or should be bought in and which should continue to be carried out in-house' (Ford et al. 1993: 211). For instance, they found that many companies seem to be much more willing to buy in more peripheral non-production functions such as cleaning and catering services than they are in their core production activities (Ford et al. 1993: 210). Furthermore, empirical observations of the reasons for make-or-buy decisions show that these are still seldom dealt with as strategic issues by firms but rather that they are based on short-term considerations (Venkatesan 1992; Ford et al. 1993). Venkatesan (1992) found that out-sourcing, for instance, is often chosen as a solution to get rid of specific problems such as lack of co-ordination between different internal functions within the firm, owing to inconsistent priorities. In addition he found that in-sourcing is often done in order to preserve jobs. Based on these observations he argued that make-or-buy decisions often seem to be made for the wrong reasons. Stuckey and White (1993) also question the reasons for make-or-buy decisions taken by firms arguing that: '. . . reasons used to justify vertical integration are often shallow and invalid. Objectives like "reducing cyclicality", "assuring market access", "moving into the high value-added stage", or "getting closer to customers" are sometimes valid, but often not' (Stuckey and White 1993: 15).

Venkatesan argues that the tools used when calculating make-or-buy alternatives are often inaccurate. He illustrates this with an empirical case, based on which he states:

> Their financial reporting systems did not help much. Most were traditional cost accounting systems for distributing overheads across all parts, rather than an activity-based system that might have provided managers with more accurate information: what parts really added value, what parts really drove overhead. In the face of distorted cost structures, sourcing decisions were made largely on emotion and myth.
>
> (Venkatesan 1992: 100)

Hence, one reason why firms have been found to fail to recognise make-or-buy problems and, when they do actually consider them still make their decisions for the wrong reasons, may be that the analytical tools are insufficient. Barreyre stresses firms' need for guidance in these matters and calls for new approaches to make-or-buy decisions:

> . . . we would like to pinpoint the fact that nowadays a new approach to the topics traditionally referred to as "vertical integration" or "make or buy" seems necessary, and that the policies devoted to the relationships with different outside partners must be considered as a dimension of corporate strategy which should not be underestimated or even ignored as it very often has been.
>
> (Barreyre 1988: 508)

Hence, make-or-buy decisions seem to be both important and difficult to analyse. There are also suggestions implying that the importance and frequency of such decisions is increasing, which is reflected in decreasing degrees of vertical integration. This may also, as argued by some authors, entail increasing technological interdependence among firms, which makes the make-or-buy situations even more complicated to analyse. The problems can be related to how the firms' own operations are affected by the decisions as well as by how they affect the relationships between the firms and their suppliers. The importance of this latter aspect implying changing content in the supplier relationships must not be neglected, since when the degree of vertical integration is reduced, the dependency on suppliers increases. Womack *et al.* identified this problem in the automobile industry:

> The make-or-buy decision that occasioned so much debate in mass production firms struck Ohno and others at Toyota as largely irrelevant, as they begun to consider obtaining components for cars and trucks. The real question was how the assembler and supplier could work together smoothly to reduce costs and improve quality, whatever formal, legal relationship they might have.
>
> (Womack *et al.* 1990: 58)

The current analytical tools applied to deal with make-or-buy decisions consist mainly of more or less sophisticated calculation methods used to assess the internal costs to be compared with the suppliers' price offers. Obviously, these are not accurate when coping with the complexities occurring in each situation, since firms do not operate in isolation, and therefore their operations cannot be analysed as independent of those undertaken by their counterparts and third parties.

THEORETICAL BACKGROUND

The division of labour has always been of fundamental concern in economic theory. Beginning with Adam Smith, ideas and the way they have developed have taken different directions over time. Here the major contributions have been divided into broad categories to enable discussion of their essentials. The discussion focuses on the division of labour or, more generally, what are seen as the structural prerequisites for efficiency within industry.

First, classical and neo-classical theory is discussed, mainly focusing on the 'market' concept in terms of the original assumptions about it and how these were gradually distorted over time.

Secondly, transaction cost analysis introducing transaction costs, or friction, in using the market is discussed in terms of the consequences of this assumption for the division of labour and its effects.

Thirdly, relationship and network analysis are discussed on the basis of the alternative view of the functioning of the market they provide.

Classical and neo-classical economic theory

Theories focusing on how activities should be divided among individuals and firms use the term division of labour. Corsi (1991: 21) distinguishes among three different, but closely related, kinds of division of labour:

1 The social division of labour which is related to the division of society into occupations and professions.

2 The intra-firm differentiation of labour which is manifested in two forms:
   (a) subdivision of labour (progressive simplification of the individual activities), and
   (b) displacement of labour (substitution of machines for workers).
3 The inter-firm specialisation of production.

This third point, which is the main theme of this book, is also referred to as the industrial division of labour and describes the scope of activities undertaken by individual firms in industrial systems.

Division of labour has been a focus of researchers' attention for a long time. Adam Smith considered the division of labour, in terms of how activities were divided among craftsmen, as the most important explanation of improvement of production and, thus, of economic growth. Departing from the social division of labour he thus stated that: 'The greatest improvement in the productive powers of labour, and the greater part of the skill, dexterity, and judgement with which it is anywhere directed, or applied, seem to have been the effects of the division of labour' (Smith 1986: 109).

With these words Adam Smith began his 'An Inquiry into the Nature and Causes of the Wealth of Nations' first published in 1776. He considered the presence of the market, being equal to the marketplace on which the results of men's labour were exchanged, as an important determinant of what was made by one craftsman and what was done by others:

> As it is the *power of exchanging* that gives occasion to the division of labour, so the extent of this division must always be limited by the extent of that power, or in other words, by the extent of the market. When the market is very small, no person can have any encouragement to dedicate himself entirely to one employment, for want of the power to exchange all that surplus part of the produce of his own labour, which is over and above his own consumption, for such parts of the produce of other men's labour as he has occasion for.
>
> (Smith 1986: 121, my emphasis)

The extent to which exchanges could take place (which Smith referred to as the market) was very much dependent upon improvements of the infrastructure which, in turn, affected the efficiency of the 'industry' which was, as Smith assumed, dependent on the division of labour:

> As by means of water-carriage a more extensive market is opened to every sort of industry than what land-carriage alone can afford it, so it is upon the sea-coast, and along the banks of navigable rivers, that industry of every kind naturally begins to *subdivide and improve* itself, and it is frequently not till a long time after those improvements extend themselves to the inland parts of the country.
>
> (Smith 1986: 122, my emphasis)

How activities are divided and organised within and among firms have, since Smith's days, been fundamental issues in economic theory. Originating from Smith's ideas, the scale and learning effects (Babbage 1832) of specialisation on a few activities was emphasised, i.e., implying a low degree of vertical integration. Hence the focus was on what affected production costs.

The dynamic aspects of Smith's theory have received less attention. According to Richardson the notion of the division of labour being limited by the extent of the market is a principle the full range and force of which may have been partially concealed by the fact that Smith discusses market extension in terms of transport improvement: '. . . unless one recognizes that the extent of the market also depends on wealth, which is in turn created by the division of labour, the dynamic character of the interaction may not be fully realized' (Richardson 1975: 352). This is in accordance with Young, who emphasised the creative, as opposed to the allocative, functions of markets in Smith's theory. He stated that '. . . the division of labour depends in large part upon the division of labour' (Young 1928: 533).

Marshall, who like Smith applied a holistic view of production as an integral part of society, drew on Smith in several respects. Among other things he elaborated on the economic consequences of specialisation, related to the possibilities of substituting routine and repetitive human works by machinery. Lately, and in this context most interestingly, Marshall has been particularly acknowledged for drawing attention to the 'external economies' of the firm. 'External economies' are described by Marshall as economies arising from an increase in the scale of production (of any kind of goods), depending on the resources of the general development of the industry, while 'internal economies' are those dependent on the resources of the individual firm. According to Marshall, 'external economies' could 'mainly be secured by the concentration of many businesses of similar character in particular localities' (Marshall 1920: 266). And, similarly to Smith, he recognised the importance of means of communication:

> . . . an increase in the aggregate scale of production of course increases those economies, which do not directly depend on size of individual houses of business. The most important of these results from the growth of correlated branches of industry which mutually assist one another, perhaps being concentrated in the same localities, but anyhow availing themselves of the modern facilities for communication offered by steam transport, by the telegraph and the printing-press. The economies arising from such sources as this . . . do not depend exclusively upon its own growth: but yet they are sure to grow rapidly and steadily with that growth; and they are sure to dwindle in some, though not in all respects, if it decays.
>
> (Marshall 1920: 317)

The firm's external organisation was seen by Marshall as part of its capital, which could be of even greater value than its tangible assets. Therefore, the accumulation of this capital over time was considered a major element in his account of the firm's development (Loasby 1991: 41). Moreover, the capabilities that are part of the external organisation also include those not controlled by any individual firm, but rather distributed among several firms

In the late nineteenth century the development of economic theory shifted away from the main concerns of Adam Smith towards what is usually referred to as 'neo-classical theory' which 'was designed not to understand the springs of economic growth and the sources of wealth but rather to analyze the allocation of known and given resources' (Langlois and Robertson 1995: 8). Swedberg describes the differences in how 'the market' was conceptualised:

> There exist many interesting differences between the concept of the market in classical political economy and the one that was to become popular around the turn of the century through the marginalist revolution. First, classical economists saw the market as synonymous with either a marketplace or a geographical area. In their eyes the market was something concrete as opposed to the abstract market of latterday economists. Second, the main emphasis in classical political economy had been on production rather than on exchange.
>
> (Swedberg (1994: 257)

The 'market' conditions that can be derived from Smith's thoughts on 'the power of exchange' were much elaborated by neo-classical economists to make them suitable for quantitative models and methods. The perfect market was assumed to ensure optimum resource allocation among firms. The neo-classical conceptualisation of the market was oriented towards competition on the market, i.e., for the market to function well, numerous sellers and buyers had to compete in order for fair prices to be set. Thus, market models of this kind are based on the assumption that there are numerous independent firms striving to maximise their profits through adapting their outputs to the prices set by the 'perfect competition' on the market.

Richardson argues that the perfect competition model, postulating universally diminishing returns to scale, presumes that increasing returns must tend to concentration and even monopoly. He contrasts this model to Smith's ideas wherein the economies of scale and specialisation were never exhausted in that an extension of the market would always permit a finer division of labour and consequent reductions in costs. Richardson therefore argues that Smith's theory of economic evolution presumes the general prevalence of increasing returns (Richardson 1975: 354). He contrasts this with neo-classical theory:

We typically start with a fixed list or set of products. A firm employs factors of production to make one of these products and we consider how unit costs vary with scale of the operation. Increasing returns are said to prevail so long as the firm can increase the output of the product, given time for adjustment, with a less than proportionate increase in total cost. If we consider a group of firms making identical products for the same market, then it is clear that, so long as any of them expe-riences increasing returns, competition must produce concentration and, in the end, monopoly.

(Richardson 1975: 354)

Obviously, the focus of neo-classical theory on the allocating function of markets makes it unsuitable to explain the development of firms and thus of industrial growth. All that is regarded as 'fixed' or 'given' in the model, together with the assumptions of perfect mobility and even perfect knowl-edge, make the model very little connected to the conditions firms are subject to. Leijonhufvud (1986: 203–4) describes the neo-classical model as a recipe for bouillabaisse where all the ingredients are dumped into a pot, heated up, and then the output is ready. Consequently, he states that 'neo-classical production theory gives us no clue to how production is actually organized'.

Transaction cost analysis

In 1937, Coase focused attention on 'the cost for using the price mech-anism', which he labelled transaction costs. The degree of vertical integration was affected when transaction costs were added to production costs in the analytical model. The implication was that the degree of vertical integration should be higher. In other words, transaction costs could explain the existence of firms. Hence, if the transaction costs had not made themselves felt, Smith's craftsmen would, according to this view, still be working by themselves, exchanging all the surplus parts of the produce of their labour on the market.

Williamson, who adopted and developed Coase's transaction cost concept for the purpose of US antitrust policy implications, included both economic and behavioural aspects in the model (Williamson 1975). Applying the transaction cost approach, researchers confining themselves to this 'new institutionalism' have been occupied with determining why and when activities are co-ordinated within or outside the firm. These two alternatives constitute governance modes referred to as 'hierarchy' and 'market'. The preferred governance mode depends, according to this model, on the transaction costs incurred in the situation. Transaction costs are assumed to be affected by two behavioural variables: *bounded rationality*, defined as the inability of economic actors to write contracts that cover all possible contingencies, and *opportunism*, defined as the rational pursuit by economic actors of their own advantage with every means at their disposal, including guile and deceit. Two additional environmental variables affecting transaction costs are *small numbers* (few firms acting on the market) and *uncertainty*, making it difficult to foresee all situations in advance when establishing contracts between actors. If bounded rationality, opportunism and small number situations prevail, and the uncertainty surrounding the situation is high, this entails high transaction costs which then calls for internalisation, i.e., hierarchy is the preferred governance mode in such situations.

Later, Williamson (1979) developed the transaction cost model to incorporate 'intermediate modes' into the analysis. The focus also changed from explaining the incentives for removing transactions from the market and organising them internally, to identifying the most economic governance mode for each abstract description of a transaction. In 1985, two governance modes had been added to the two previous ones as Williamson declared that he was: 'now persuaded that transactions in the middle range' existed and had to be incorporated into the analysis. These two governance modes are referred to as 'trilateral governance', which involves action by mediating third parties, and 'bilateral governance', which involves 'relational contracting' between firms. Trilateral governance, it is argued, is needed when transactions are occasional, and assets are specific to a medium or high extent. Third party assistance is needed to resolve disputes and evaluate performance. Purchasing of customised equipment and construction of plants are examples of such transactions and the architect is mentioned as an example of a relatively independent third party (Williamson 1985: 74–5). Bilateral governance is considered the preferred mode if the frequency of transactions is high and there is a mixed investment characteristic present, i.e., asset specificity is present, but not to a high extent. As an example of such transactions, Williamson refers to purchasing of customised material. Together with small numbers, uncertainty and opportunism, previously recognised by him as affecting the predominating mode of governance, the *frequency of transactions* and the importance of *asset specificity* (which refers to assets that are less transferable to other uses and users) were added as variables. If the frequency of transactions is high and there is asset specificity, hierarchy is the preferred governance mode, i.e., the activity should be organised within the firm. The reason for this, according to Williamson, is that:

> as human and physical assets become more specialised to a single use, and hence less transferable to other uses, economies of scale can be as fully realised by the buyer as by an outside supplier. The choice of organising mode then turns entirely on which mode has superior

adaptive properties. As discussed . . . vertical integration will ordinarily appear in such circumstances.

(Williamson 1985: 78)

The advantage of vertical integration is, moreover, considered to be that adaptations can be made sequentially without involvement of other parties. Langlois and Robertson (1995: 36) refer to an early work by Teece in which he elaborated on the co-ordination problem: 'If there is a high degree of interdependence among successive stages of production, and if occasions for adaptations are unpredictable yet common, coordinated responses may be difficult to secure if the separate stages are operated independently'. Hence, co-ordination within the firm is preferred when contingencies cannot be predicted perfectly in advance. Langlois and Robertson (1995: 37) argue that this is in fact the general explanation of vertical integration, and that basically all other transaction cost explanations are derived from this argument. Therefore, Langlois and Robertson, who view the Coasian transaction costs as short-term phenomena, have introduced the 'dynamic transaction cost' concept defined as 'the costs of persuading, negotiating, coordinating and teaching outside suppliers'. Langlois and Robertson (1995: 35) also describe dynamic transaction costs as 'the costs of not having the capabilities you need when you need them'. Like the Coasian transaction costs, these may result in vertical integration. Also, they take Teece's suggestion a bit further by introducing systemic innovation as opposed to autonomous innovation:

As Teece suggests, the cost of coordinating among stages would be greatest when there is a high degree of interdependence among the relevant stages of production. But more than mere interdependence is necessary: the interdependence must be such that a change in one stage of production requires a corresponding change in one or more distinct stages. That is, it must be systemic.

(Langlois and Robertson 1995: 37).

Langlois and Robertson argue that transaction costs are short-term phenomena, since 'frictions' are considered to be transient, and that production costs alone tell us a great deal about the organisation of economy. Dynamic transaction costs are, however, considered needed to deal with the boundaries of the firm and the nature of contractual relationships among firms, 'But, the modern focus on transaction costs, salutary as it has been, has nonetheless put into background the richness of the classical cost-of-production theory' (Langlois and Robertson 1995: 25–6).

The transaction cost approach has received an abundance of attention, and therefore also of criticism (see for example Englander 1988; Loasby 1991; Richardson 1995). A question posed by Richardson (1995: 1494) may illustrate one of the main points: 'Why do they seem implicitly to believe that conspiracy rather than confusion is generally at the root of market failure, and tend therefore to appraise the efficiency of alternative structures in that light?'

In the context of this book there are other critical points of concern in the transaction cost approach which have more to do with structure than behaviour. Within transaction cost analysis, relationships among firms are basically regarded as market imperfections. The market and the hierarchy are seen as 'pure' governance modes, while the relationship mode is seen as intermediate. The market is assumed to co-ordinate wholly independent activities while interdependent activities should be subject to internal co-ordination. Now, if we consider the relationship mode as offering co-ordination of activities 'between' these extremes, the question is what this 'between' may actually be. For analytical purposes relationships between firms, co-ordinating interdependent activities across firm boundaries, are considered here as a form of co-ordination in its own right and not as a 'between' mode. This is in line with Richardson's argument that: 'The dichotomy between firm and market, between directed and spontaneous co-ordination, is misleading; it ignores the institutional fact of co-operation and assumes away the distinct method of co-ordination that this can provide' (Richardson 1972: 895).

Other authors also emphasise the importance of understanding and analysing relationship or network governance, as it is also known, as *different* from markets and hierarchies:

> In terms of transaction cost theory, the network mode offers firms a new way of handling market imperfections, in particular those related to innovation. In certain circumstances, this mode is superior to both markets and hierarchies, but it is so because it is *different* from both and not somewhere 'in between'.
>
> (OECD report 1992: 78)

A consequence of the interdependence among activities co-ordinated by relationships is that relationships themselves are interconnected, and thus embedded in larger contexts. Contrary to the view of transaction cost analysts this makes individual relationships (and even more so the individual transactions involved) unsuitable to isolate for analytical purposes.

The problems brought up above reflect some of the main differences in view between the transaction cost approach and the network approach, which is further discussed below. The differences may largely be explained by the different purposes for which the models have been developed, and the consequent levels at which analysis is applied. It is, however, important to notice that these differences in view have far-reaching consequences in terms of analysing the organisation of industrial activities.

Relationship and network analysis

During the late 1960s and early 1970s three researchers were questioning, independently of one another, the previously accepted fact that activities were co-ordinated either within firms or through market exchange (Johanson 1966; Blois 1971; Richardson 1972). The concepts they used to describe the phenomenon they had observed were business relationship (Johanson 1966), vertical quasi-integration (Blois 1971), and inter-firm co-operation (Richardson 1972). Blois defined vertical quasi-integration as situations 'where some firms are gaining the advantages of vertical integration without assuming the risks or rigidity of ownership' (Blois 1971: 253). Rather than dealing with issues traditionally considered essential by economists, e.g., the division of labour, their interest focused on relationships between firms. This seems mainly to have been a reaction to simplified underlying assumptions about the functioning of firms and markets put forward by other models.

Although the co-ordination properties of relationships have not been much elaborated since they were first 'identified', relationships among firms as social phenomena have been studied extensively. A number of empirical studies of relationships between firms and their interconnection within industrial networks were undertaken during the 1980s (see Håkansson (ed.) 1982; Turnbull and Valla (eds) 1986; Ford (ed.) 1990; Axelsson and Easton (eds) 1992). Studies in this research tradition, referred to here as the 'network approach', have mainly focused on dynamic aspects of industrial systems, especially concerning the exchange and adaptation processes within them (Johanson and Mattsson 1987).

Some observations from the empirical studies of relationships regarding their general features are the following:

- *Continuity:* the major relationships of a company are often long lasting.
- *Complexity* in terms of the range of contacts among individuals from the interacting firms both regarding the number of participants and their functions within the firms.
- *Low degree of formalisation:* formal agreements have been found seldom to be used as a means of handling uncertainties regarding the exchange among the parties in relationships. Instead, trust seems to be more relied on.
- *Symmetry in resources and initiative:* both parties usually control resources which are of importance to the counterpart and both parties are also active in the maintenance and development of the relationship.
- *Adaptations:* both parties make adaptations, for instance, technical, administrative and/or logistical, in order to function better vis-à-vis one another.
- *Both co-operation and conflicts are present* and handled within the relationships, which usually entails constructive solutions to problems.

- *Connectedness:* relationships are connected in different ways and to different extents, not least concerning their technical content.

Apart from studies undertaken to investigate the nature of the major relationships in which firms are involved, other kinds of studies have led to observations of more or less closely knit networks of firms built up on the basis of relationships. Studies focusing on technological development (Håkansson 1989; Waluszewski 1989; Lundgren 1994; Carlsson and Jacobsson 1992) have identified technological networks or systems and important mechanisms within them. The importance of the connectedness among relationships and the heterogeneity or variety provided by networks is especially stressed.

Contrary to the transaction cost approach, legal frameworks of transactions are, in line with empirical evidence, considered less important within the network approach. In addition, the exact boundaries of individual organisations are considered unclear. Both approaches focus on dyadic units (relationships and transactions respectively) but industrial systems, when seen as networks, are made up of many more or less interdependent, and thus embedded, relationships. Consequently, if one dyadic change is made, other relationships are affected. Thus, although the efficiency of a particular relationship may increase as a result of a certain change, the overall efficiency may be reduced as a result of negative impacts on other relationships. Owing to the interdependence among activities performed by different actors, not only transaction or exchange activities are affected by the counterparts to the individual firm. Rather, internal activities are also seen as parts of a wider context. As such they cannot be changed without consequences for others.

Viewing firms as social units, the network approach lies closer to social exchange theory than the transaction cost approach, which is rooted in neo-classical economics (Johanson and Mattsson 1987; Nooteboom 1993). However, the economic consequences of relationships have been given increasing attention in recent studies of industrial networks (Eriksson and Åsberg 1994, Håkansson and Snehota 1995). The importance of developing an 'economic theory of networks' is stressed in an OECD report:

> Although the time is ripe for the development of a full-fledged 'economic theory of networks' most studies are still couched in the framework of the Coase-Williamson theory of markets and hierarchies. ... A 'markets' and 'hierarchies' framework may hinder economists and technology policy makers from properly identifying the theoretical implications of the present diversity of organisational designs.
>
> (OECD report 1992: 77–8)

An economic theory of networks, however, necessarily entails greater complexity than transaction cost analysis. The greater complexity stems from the various connections among all impacting variables making it impossible to isolate, for instance, individual transactions or relationships. Rather, the connectedness and the complex dynamics within networks resulting from it need be included.

Hence, researchers from different disciplines and countries have identified network-like organisations on industrial 'markets'. This differs greatly from the traditional view of markets and the behaviour of firms on these markets. Basically, firms in networks have been found to interact actively with one another. The counterparts are thereby known and specific, rather than being numerous anonymous sellers and buyers. This is further emphasised by the importance of individual relationships, which is reflected in high concentration ratios on both the selling and buying sides of industrial companies. In a study of 123 medium-sized Swedish companies, the ten largest customers were found to account for 72 per cent of the sales on the average, while the ten largest suppliers accounted for 70 per cent of the purchase value (Håkansson 1989).

Turning to the theoretical modelling of these phenomena, there are certain differences. Some general models of co-ordination of activities in society and/or industry incorporate the three types of co-ordination: markets, hierarchies and networks (Richardson 1972, Thompsson *et al.* 1991, Piore 1992). In general, network governance has been a much less recognised co-ordination form than market and hierarchical governance. However, Piore regards markets and hierarchies as extreme forms of governance, i.e., the network mode is considered the natural form of organisation, while Richardson and Thompsson *et al.* regard them as three complementary models of co-ordination featured by different governance mechanisms. Hence, there is great variation among models addressing modes of governance:

> The point is that there is no single and totally accepted view of how the market works, of how hierarchy works, or how networks work to 'produce' coordination. Each of these approaches represents a contested territory where different and often competing claims are made as to the proper understanding of their respective coordinative effects.
>
> (Thompsson *et al.* 1991: 4)

Therefore, it is difficult to address a particular model as *the* network approach. However, as a point of departure for this frame of reference the network model presented by Håkansson (1987) has been chosen as it encompasses concepts which have been found to be valuable building blocks for description and analysis of how firms work within technologically complex contexts.

The network model is based on three components: actors, activities and resources. Each one of these components is seen as dependent on the other two (see Figure 1.1).

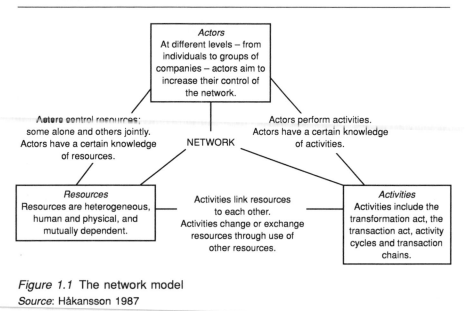

Figure 1.1 The network model
Source: Håkansson 1987

Actors are defined by their performance of activities and their control over resources. Since activities and resources are connected to those of other actors in various ways, actors have connections to other actors. In the network, a certain actor has an identity, because of its unique combination of activities and resources.

Activities are undertaken by actors who activate their resources in a process in which other resources are refined. The activities undertaken by actors are not carried out in isolation as their activities are linked to those undertaken by other actors. Hence, an important feature of the activities is that they are enacted (Weick 1969) in the sense that actors develop and organise their activities in response to how their counterparts, such as customers and suppliers, perform and organise theirs.

The activities undertaken by an actor are referred to as production (or transformation) activities, and those undertaken between actors are referred to as exchange (or transaction) activities. One important function of the exchange activities is that they co-ordinate interdependence among production activities undertaken by firms whose activities are interrelated. There may be sequential dependence, since some activities must be undertaken before others, but there is also mutual dependence, for instance because the results of two activities are going to be used together.

An actor controls various resources such as manpower, equipment, plants, knowledge and financial resources. The basic feature characterising resources is that they are heterogeneous, which means that their value or utility depends on the resources with which they are combined. Because of this, knowledge and learning about resources are important to actors. Resource control can either be direct in the sense that the company possesses the resource (or the right to use it), or indirect by gaining access to it by a relationship to a counterpart in possession of it. The relationships an actor is involved in may therefore also be regarded as resources, since they constitute valuable bridges to accessing resources possessed by other actors. Hence, the problems, or costs, perceived by transaction cost econ omists in handling systemic innovations (Langlois and Robertson 1995) in relationships are not seen in the same way by network researchers. Rather, relationships are considered necessary to innovation.

The heterogeneity assumption is based on the work of Alchian and Demsetz, who explain the existence of firms by a distinction between homogenous and heterogeneous resources. The value of homogenous resources is independent of what other resources they are combined with (an assumption usually held by economists), while the value of heterogeneous resources is dependent on these other resources: 'the firm is a specialised surrogate for a market for team use of inputs; it provides superior (i.e., cheaper) collection and collation of knowledge about heterogeneous resources' (Alchian and Demsetz 1972: 794). Therefore: 'Efficient production with heterogeneous resources is a result not of having *better* resources but in *knowing more accurately* the relative productive performance of those resources' (ibid.: 793).

However, while Alchian and Demsetz regard heterogeneity as a means of explaining the existence of firms (which is very different from the transaction cost explanation), Håkansson (1992) argues that networks as a form of governance feature the right mechanisms to achieve heterogeneity since they offer a combination of stability and variation. In studies of technological development (see Waluszewski 1989; Lundgren 1994) the understanding of the behaviour of companies, especially regarding their technological considerations, has been extended beyond the economic models focusing solely on the costs associated with production and exchange. If the resources controlled by firms are assumed to be heterogeneous, identification and understanding of the values and benefits resulting from the various activities undertaken by firms can also be incorporated into the analysis.

While relationships have been regarded by transaction cost economists as a form of governance used when being cost effective, the variety and multidimensionality of the content of relationships have not been a focus of their attention. To capture the large variation within relationships, Håkansson and Snehota (1995) describe them as having two dimensions: content and function. The content is characterised by three layers, which are the main elements of the network model, i.e., activities, resources and actors. The activity layer is related to productivity, the resource layer to innovativity and the actor layer to identity. The functions of relationships are also three-fold: the individual actors, the dyad and the network (third parties) may all be affected by a relationship. The three functions of a relationship stem from the embedded nature of relationships as they are elements in a network and, as such, interconnected. Hence, a relationship not only affects the two parties involved in it but also other (third) parties in the network. The key attributes of a relationship in terms of its function for the dyad are described and analysed as its content regarding activity links, resource ties and actor bonds.

A relationship may contain resource ties in that exchange of, access to, and/or combinations of resources may be ingredients of a relationship. Through relationships, it becomes possible for individual actors to mobilise resources which may affect their innovativity. As a relationship can be regarded as a resource in itself, it must be looked after and utilised in an efficient way, like other assets of a company.

Important features regarding the bonds between actors are mutual commitment and assumed identity of the counterpart, which stem from past experience. The creation of bonds and the shaping of identities can be described as a learning process in which the perceptions of the counterparts are developed. The organised network of actors, being the aggregated structure of actors and actor bonds, is undetermined in the sense that it is not related to some overriding purpose for the structure as a whole. This is a consequence of relationships arising for various reasons.

Every individual firm performs activities and co-ordinates these activities in a certain way. Activity linking entails co-ordination of the activities performed by the parties involved in a relationship (Dubois and Håkansson 1997). If or when the internal activity structures within the two companies change, the links between activities may have to be adapted somehow. The activities of the two parties are, hence, inter-dependent in different ways and to different extents. Based on this interdependence, the linking of activities can be utilised to create unique performance. The individual actor's performance in terms of productivity is therefore affected, through the activity links, both by its own activities and by the activities of its counterparts.

In traditional economic models, economic efficiency regards resource utilisation in terms of given resources for given purposes. Hence, efficiency is the input–output ratio in resource transformation. Håkansson and Snehota (1995) stress the need for a broader concept of economy in which resource utilisation is not confined to exploitation of *given* resources for *given* purposes. Based on findings about the nature of relationships, impor-tant aspects include change and improvement in resource use, the scope of activities and the knowledge and capacity of actors. The resources controlled and used by economic actors may therefore be regarded as given at a certain moment but, as they interact, new resources and resource combinations are developed over time. Also, the purpose for which the resources are used changes over time as the activities carried out are interdependent and arbitrary in a relationship perspective. New activities may be added to the activities already undertaken by an actor and the activities may be interlinked in new ways. Hence:

> the resources are used for activities the scope and purpose of which is not 'given', by actors whose identities, perceptions and intentions are never fully 'given'. While the single actors pursue purposes they see very much as given, the 'purpose' of resource utilization cannot be seen as generally given.'
>
> (Håkansson and Snehota 1995: 383–4)

Therefore, the critical question is considered to be related to the dynamics, i.e., how resource utilisation changes and develops.

When activities are reorganised among firms, the conditions for resource utilisation change. This, in turn, has an impact on efficiency. Analysing efficiency as a result of changes in resource use can then either be done, *a priori*, in relation to the actor dimension or the activity dimension. Traditional models have usually taken the actor dimension as their point of departure. This book focuses on the activities undertaken by firms and how these activities are interrelated as the platform for understanding division of labour among firms and thus the structural prerequisites for efficiency within activity structures.

By focusing on the activity dimension, the division of labour among firms may be seen as a matter of how activities are organised by and within firms who are interrelated in different ways in terms of how their activities are linked. Thereby, the activity structures, including the activities undertaken within the firms and the ways these activities are interrelated, can be identified and analysed.

Previous studies undertaken within the network framework have mainly been concerned with technical development. Owing to that focus, the approach of these studies has mainly been concentrated on the actor and the resource dimensions. That is, network studies focusing on the activity dimension, which is needed when dealing with the division of labour, seem to be lacking. To provide a basis for further discussion of activity interdependence and the forms of co-ordination of these activities in industrial systems, we now turn to models addressing the 'lowest' level in the system, i.e., the individual activities.

Chapter 2

An activity based framework

TOWARDS AN ACTIVITY BASED FRAMEWORK
TO DEAL WITH DIVISION OF LABOUR

Stigler (1951) is one of the few authors who have approached the division of labour using the activities undertaken by firms as the main unit of analysis. Questioning the importance of transaction costs and claiming that they are not necessarily less within a firm than between firms, he drew on Smith's notion of the division of labour as limited by the extent of the market. He concluded that: 'Smith's theorem suggests that vertical disintegration is the typical development in growing industries, vertical integration in declining industries' (Stigler 1951: 189). This conclusion has recently been criticised by Langlois and Robertson (1995: 21) who argue that it 'is unwarranted and, if taken narrowly, is probably exactly backwards'.

One interesting aspect of the analysis, however, is that Stigler focused attention on the activities undertaken by firms when elaborating on the different cost functions by which the activities are characterised. The cost functions were used to analyse the changing degrees of vertical integration in industries. In doing this he also questioned the need for a theory of vertical integration except as a part of a theory of the activities of a firm.

> The firm is usually viewed as purchasing a series of inputs, from which it obtains one or more salable products. . . . For our purpose it is better to view the firm as engaging in a series of distinct operations: purchasing and storing materials; transforming materials into semifinished products and semifinished products into finished products; storing and selling the outputs; extending credit to buyers etc. That is, we partition the firm not among the markets in which it buys inputs but among the functions or processes which constitute the scope of activity.
>
> (Stigler 1951: 57)

However, like most theorists dealing with the division of labour, he held on to the dichotomy of firms and markets. That is, he disregarded the possibility of co-ordination of interdependent activities across firm boundaries.

Similar to Stigler, Richardson focused on the activities undertaken by firms, but in the framework he developed for analysis of co-ordination among these activities, all three forms of governance were included. Two activity concepts are used in this framework regarding how the co-ordination can be handled: complementary and similar activities. Complementary activities are defined as activities 'representing different phases of a process of production and require in some way or another to be co-ordinated' (Richardson 1972: 889). This definition of complementarity could, thus, be related to the vertical or sequential dependence among activities. Thereby Richardson's definition differs from the more general, and less contextual one presented, for instance, by Milgrom and Roberts (1992: 543): 'two activities are complementary if the profit or value created by doing both is greater than the sum of the individual profits from doing just one or the other'.

Furthermore, activities may, according to Richardson, be closely complementary if there is a need to 'match not the aggregate output of a general-purpose input with the aggregate output for which it is needed but of particular activities' (Richardson 1972: 891). Hence, close complementarity exists when an activity is directed to another specific activity. Another way of putting this is that the results of closely complementary activities are restricted to particular purposes and, hence, cannot be used for other purposes.

Similar activities are activities which 'require the same capability for their undertaking' (Richardson 1972: 889), i.e., a particular resource is used to undertake more than one activity. Similarity among activities thus causes what we may call horizontal dependence among activities sharing common resources. For instance, several assembly operations resulting in different products may be handled by the same personnel and equipment. Moreover, complementary activities may also be similar, that is when two or several activities undertaken in a sequence require the same resources or capabilities.

Using this classification, Richardson suggests that co-ordination can be effected in three ways: internally within one firm (which he calls directed co-ordination); by co-operation between firms; or through market transactions. There would, according to Richardson, be no limit to the extent to which co-ordination could be effected within one organisation if it could be assumed that the scale on which an activity was undertaken did not affect its efficiency, and that no special capabilities were ever required by the firm undertaking it. Hence, the scope for co-ordination of activities within firms is narrowly circumscribed by the existence of economies of scale and the fact that complementary activities need not be similar (Richardson 1972: 890). In a recent article Richardson added another activity concept to his previous framework – 'systematic closely complementary' activities – to explain the scope of internal co-ordination. These are not clearly defined but introduced by stating that 'a stage will be reached, as the number of related activities increases, at which overall design becomes indispensable' (Richardson 1995: 1494).

As for co-ordination by market transactions, this may, according to Richardson, be relied upon when:

> there is no attempt to match complementary activities *ex ante* by deliberately co-ordinating the corresponding plans; salvation is then sought, not through reciprocal undertakings, but on that stability with which aggregates, by the law of large numbers, are providentally endowed.
>
> (Richardson 1972: 891)

The third way to cope with the co-ordination of activities is through relationship, or co-operation as Richardson refers to it, through which co-ordination is achieved when two or more organisations agree to match their related plans in advance. This may be the most efficient form of governance in situations characterised by close complementarity and dissimilarity among the activities undertaken by two firms:

> This co-ordination cannot be left entirely to direction within firms because the activities are dissimilar, and cannot be left to market forces in that it requires not the balancing of the aggregate supply of something with the aggregate demand for it but rather the matching, both qualitative and quantitative, of individual enterprise plans.
>
> (Richardson 1972: 892)

In these situations, there is mutual dependence between the production activities undertaken by the buyer and the seller both in terms of what is produced (which is thus specific to each customer) and in terms of production volume. When firms buy and/or manufacture products which are specifically adapted by or to a counterpart, the technical issue of combining resources and activities also becomes an economic issue depending on the firms' counterparts and the activities undertaken by them. Hence, to understand the complexities of structures of interdependent activities, the activities and resources, considered in economic models as 'internal' to firms, must be viewed in their contexts as they are dependent upon activities and resources performed and controlled by others. Taking the complexities caused by interdependency across firm boundaries into account, further understanding of the effects of the 'power of exchange' coined by Smith (1986), and the 'external economies' of firms introduced by Marshall (1920), on the division of labour, may be provided.

ACTIVITIES, ACTIVITY CHAINS AND ACTIVITY STRUCTURES

In the framework introduced in this chapter the activities undertaken by firms, and the ways they are organised within and across firm boundaries, are the primary building blocks. Before we deal with how the activities are divided among firms, within the organised activity structures in which they are embedded, the individual activities and the way they are organised vis-à-vis one another must be elaborated.

The outcome of each individual activity is referred to as a *product*. For instance, the activity may be cutting of steel plate. The product resulting from that activity is a steel plate cut into a certain format. In order to be able to perform this activity, a steel plate, which is the result of a prior activity, is needed. Furthermore, the cutting activity precedes another activity, e.g., bending. Hence, a chain of three activities appears: the production of steel plate, the cutting, and the bending of the cut steel plate (see Figure 2.1). Thus, individual activities are interrelated in *activity chains*, in which the individual activities are undertaken in a certain sequence.

If we assume that the steel plate constituting the product of the first activity is cut into three different formats and that these cut steel plates, in turn, are bent into different shapes to suit different purposes, then three activity chains emanate from the first product. These chains are illustrated in Figure 2.2.

If we focus on the first chain starting with activities A, B1 and C1 in Figure 2.2 these eventually end up in an excavator. We may refer to the excavator as the *end product* of the activities. The activities following the bending activity (C1) may be welding (of several cut and bent steel plates), painting and assembly. Some of the activities constituting the activity structure of the excavator are particularly adjusted to the excavator, such as the cutting and bending activities (B1 and C1), while other activities, such as the production of steel plates (activity A), are not.

Looking at the second activity chain emanating from activity A, the first activities adjusted to the end product – which is a car in this case – are the

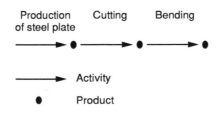

Figure 2.1 Three activities organised into an activity chain

cutting activity B2 and the bending activity C2. The next activity in the chain may be an assembly activity wherein the cut and bent steel plate is mounted with other parts of the car. The activity following may be painting, and then a second assembling activity may appear followed by final painting.

The third activity chain starting in activity A in Figure 2.2 is part of an activity structure resulting in a fork lift truck. The bending activity C3 may in this case be followed by a painting activity which, in turn, is followed by an assembly activity. Lastly, test driving and final adjustments of the truck may be undertaken.

Hence, in order to define or delimit an activity structure for analytical purposes, we may specify a certain *end product*. The activity structure thus becomes an aggregate of all individual activities needed for producing the specified end product. Within that *end product related activity structure*, individual activities and activity chains can be identified. However, an individual activity may be a part of several end product related activity structures, and therefore it cannot be analysed in only one context but must be dealt with as a part of all activity structures in which it is embedded.

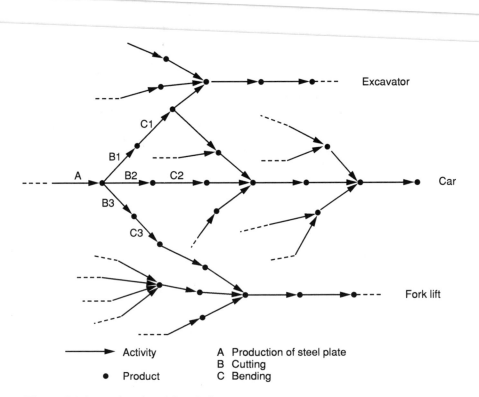

Figure 2.2 Interrelated activity chains

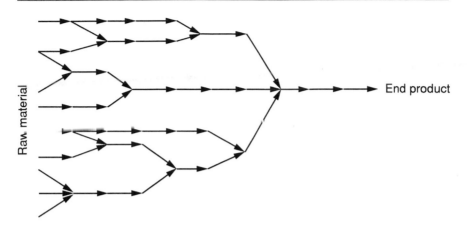

Figure 2.3 The principle of an end product related activity structure

If we imagine the activities necessary for the creation of an end product and we start with the raw materials used in the process, it could, at a simple level, look something like Figure 2.3. Here the focus is on the activities that transform the material.

The transformation activities can be said to refine the material. Different materials may be merged, they may be shaped by activities such as casting, cutting or milling, and they may be put together, for instance by welding and assembling activities, and so forth. In Figure 2.3 we can see how the sequence in which the activities are performed forms them into chains of activities which result in a certain end product. In addition, owing to the merging of activity chains in the activity structure, there are also parallel connections, for instance between activities resulting in components which are subsequently assembled. These are the basic structural features of how activities are interrelated. At any given moment these activities and the structure they form can be considered as given. At any moment, the activities are undertaken by different firms, thus resulting in a certain division of labour, but this existing division of labour is not the only possible one. Rather, the activities resulting in a certain end product could be organised in any number of ways. If we consider the forms the division of labour may take, an obvious question is how this particular division of labour, of all the possible alternatives, can be explained. Figure 2.4 illustrates two of the numerous ways in which an end product related activity structure may be divided among firms.

Economies of specialisation related to scale and learning are naturally important explanations of why the activities are performed by different specialising firms. All firms in the system or structure also have many other customers and suppliers. The basis for the economies of specialisation is then

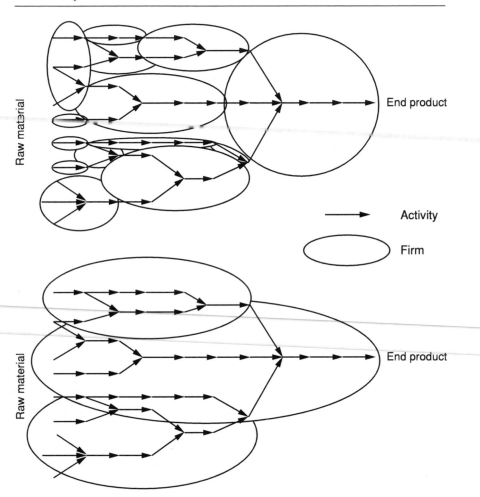

Figure 2.4 Two examples of the division of labour within an end product related activity structure

easily understood if each firm performs activities resulting in some standard product(s) offered to large numbers of customers. The advantages of firms specialising in some transformation activities are apparent from this point of view (see Figure 2.5).

In addition to the transformation (or production) activities undertaken by the respective firms, the activities needed in order to handle the exchange between them also have to be taken into account when introducing firms into the structure. The transaction or exchange activities can be seen as connecting the transformation activities performed by the different firms in Figure 2.5.

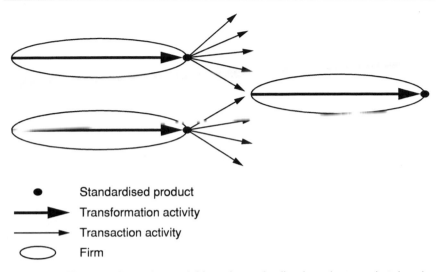

●   Standardised product

━━━▶   Transformation activity

─────▶   Transaction activity

⬭   Firm

Figure 2.5 The transformation activities of standardised products undertaken by three firms and the transaction activities connecting them

The transformation activities performed by these firms result in standardised products and can therefore be performed independently. The independence is based on the fact that no specific adjustments of the firms' transformation activities towards the customers are made in this situation. Hence, the efficiency of this solution is based on the fact that all the firms exchange products, produced on a large scale – i.e., they all benefit from the advantages of specialisation. Therefore, when the activities performed by a firm exchanging its products through market exchange are analysed, they may be seen and analysed as a whole. If the companies operating under these conditions manufacture several different products, this is usually explained as economies of scope, which are defined by Panzar and Willig (1981: 268) as 'cost savings which result from the scope (rather than scale) of the enterprise' when it is 'less costly to combine two or more product lines in one firm than to produce them separately'. This definition of economies of scope thus focuses on what happens within the firms as related to the resulting products (although the situation becomes more complex, owing to the need to co-ordinate the activity chains resulting in the different products) since there is no interdependence between these chains and the customers' activities. Teece (1982: 48–54) identifies four classes of scope economies:

1 Indivisible but non-specialised physical capital as a common input into two or more products.
2 Indivisible specialised physical capital as a common input to two or more products.

3 Human capital as a common input to two or more products.
4 External economies.

Although Teece deals with the specificities as product related and the external economies as related to market transactions, his classification may well be used here with reference instead to specific counterparts and the resources that are activated by activities directed to them.

For analytical purposes we concentrate below on economies of scale related to individual activities, and so the firm-level concept of scope economies as such is not contemplated further. The impact of what Teece refers to as 'imperfectly divisible factors' is, however, dealt with, as these structural restraints can be handled differently when taking relationships into account as opposed to regarding them as internal to firms.

Let us return to the end product related activity structure illustrated in Figure 2.3: consider the situations where some products are not standardised but need features specific to the particular end product. What would then be more efficient about organising these activities outside the end product manufacturing firm? In order to understand the division of labour when it is not solely based on economies of specialisation related to the whole operation of firms, we have to examine an activity structure to explore how activities are related to each other within and between the boundaries of individual firms.

DIVISION OF LABOUR AND EFFICIENCY OF ACTIVITY STRUCTURES

If an end product related activity structure is defined as all the activities needed to create a particular end product and as the way these activities are organised at a certain point in time, the activities have to be co-ordinated within that activity structure – both within the firms involved and among them. Richardson's analysis helps to clarify important reasons for the division of labour within an activity structure, and may be summarised and illustrated by an example of a chain of activities performed in a row by three different firms (see Figure 2.6).

Activity A, undertaken by the first firm in the row, results in a standardised product which is co-ordinated, by market exchange, with other activities (one of which is activity B), which are both complementary and dissimilar with regard to activity A. The middle firm undertakes two closely complementary activities (B and C). The reason these two activities are co-ordinated within the firm, according to Richardson's analysis, is that they are either similar (i.e., the same resources can be used for both activities) or they are dissimilar, with no economies of scale connected to the utilisation of special capabilities or resources. In the latter case, i.e., when the activities (B and C) are dissimilar with no connected economies

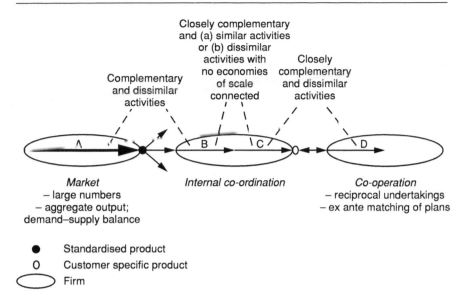

Figure 2.6 A chain of activities co-ordinated in three different ways

of scale, it would, according to Richardson's analysis, be equally efficient to perform activity C in the next firm in the row. Then why does the last firm not undertake activity C, which is not only closely complementary to activity B but also to activity D which is already performed within its boundary?

More than twenty years after his first article on the subject Richardson added the concept of 'systematic close complementary activities' to deal with this problem (Richardson 1995). Activities subject to systematic close complementarity can only be co-ordinated by internal direction, i.e., organised within the firm. Systematic close complementarity can thus explain why activities B and C need be undertaken within one firm.

For the purpose of this book it is argued that the recognition of *the connection* between close complementarity and similarity, already present in Richardson's framework, is a better solution. This connection, between what we refer to as horizontal interdependence (activities subject to similarity) and vertical interdependence (activities subject to close complementarity), is a much more powerful explanation, and one that leads much further, than the explanation based on systematic close complementarity.

Let us focus on the explanation provided by the connection between horizontal and vertical interdependence. If we consider the two activities (B and C) undertaken by the firm in the middle, and assume that this firm's output consists of more than one customer specific product, it seems logical that activities B and C are co-ordinated within this firm if the activities

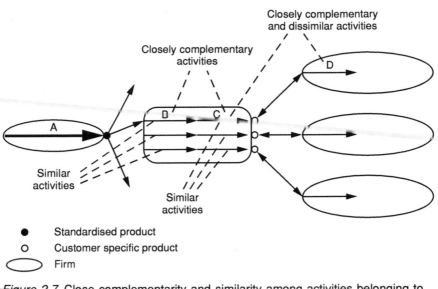

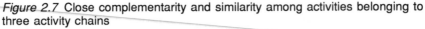

● Standardised product
○ Customer specific product
⬭ Firm

Figure 2.7 Close complementarity and similarity among activities belonging to three activity chains

resulting in the other customised products are similar in some respects with regard to activities B and C (see Figure 2.7). This will be the case when some of the resources activated by the activities can be shared among them to some extent. In other words, this may be an efficient solution if this firm's customers have similar needs with reference to the activities required to satisfy them. Then a fair assumption would be that what can be done for each customer in terms of efficiency is dependent upon, or a function of, what is done for the other customers. And therefore, with reference to the resources used, this is dependent on (a) the degree of similarity of the customers' needs (in terms of all activities directed to them), and (b) the economies of scale that can be achieved. Hence, even if there is no aggregate output but rather the firm manufactures products specific to each of its customers, it is possible to achieve economies of scale in individual activities or in parts of chains consisting of closely complementary activities (see Figure 2.7). Teece's definition of scope economies may thus be applied in this new context. However, to capture the efficiency of structures in which there is interdependence across firm boundaries, the analysis of the economies of scale and specialisation need be carried out at the activity level and not at the firm level.

To analyse interdependence among activities, three interrelated dimensions need be included (see Figure 2.8). First, an individual activity is part of an activity chain wherein the activities are vertically interdependent. This is illustrated in Figure 2.8 by the chain in which activity B1 is a part:

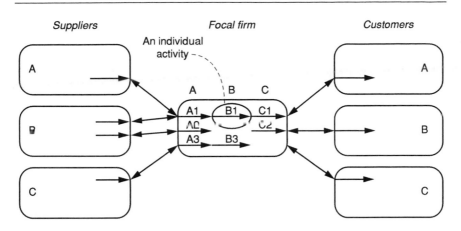

Figure 2.8 An individual activity in its context

the activities undertaken by suppliers A and B, the activity A1 undertaken prior to B1 and the activity undertaken directly after it, activity C1,
which are both undertaken within the same firm, and the activity undertaken by customer A, are all included in the chain.

Secondly, horizontal interdependence among activities may be created
through connecting similar activities belonging to different end product
related activity structures. An individual activity may thus be horizontally
interdependent to similar activities if they activate common resources to
some extent. For example, activity B1 may share certain resources with
activity B3.

Thirdly, the individual activity is one among all those undertaken within
the boundary of a particular firm. Activity B1 is related to activities A1–3,
B3 and C1–2 in this way.

It is important to notice how the three dimensions are interrelated.
Individual activities are interlinked both in terms of common resource
utilisation and also in sequence, which means that a change of one individual activity may impact in very different ways, and to different extents, on
other activities. Individual activities are parts of activity chains connected to
one another within the boundaries of a certain firm. A change in a chain
directed towards one particular customer may affect the activities directed
towards other customers. This may, in turn, affect third parties through the
connections that may exist among these activities and others. The efficiency
with which activities can be undertaken is thus dependent upon the extent
to which resource sharing is obtained. This is, however, only a static
measure. But the way activities are organised also influences the possibilities and incentives for developing the resources, which impacts on the
dynamics of activity structures. The resources activated by the activities can
be related to the three dimensions of analysis.

The first dimension of analysis concerns activity chains that cut across several firms. A company has resources in its purchasing, production and marketing functions to co-ordinate these activity chains. The resources needed to handle the activity links include knowledge of the activities to which the individual firm's activities are connected. The joint ability to co-ordinate the activity chains among the firms involved sequentially and in parallel is therefore also an important resource. This resource may, when interdependent activities are organised across firm boundaries, be attributable to the interaction among the firms involved rather than to the individual firms.

The second dimension of analysis concerns how the individual activities are interconnected by resource sharing. The resources activated may consist of equipment of different kinds such as machinery, tools, personnel with more or less specific skills, materials consumed in the process, such as electrodes, etc. A set of resources is thus connected to each and every activity, although it may to some extent be utilised by several activities, e.g., activity A and B in Figure 2.8 may be operated by the same personnel.

The third dimension of analysis is the whole operation of a firm and, in the view presented, this dimension encompasses two sub-dimensions: one related to the horizontal and the other to the vertical interdependence among the activities undertaken by the firm. Co-ordination of the two sub-dimensions therefore becomes essential. The management resources necessary to operate a firm is dependent on the scope of the two sub-dimensions together. Co-ordination entails both the connection of the activity chains directed towards different customers, in order to capture and develop similarities among the individual activities, and also the creation of the unique features the different customers require. The overall efficiency or productivity of each individual firm is therefore determined through this co-ordination.

It is necessary to understand how activities and activity chains are interconnected in an activity structure in order to analyse change in that structure. The discussion has so far dealt with given activities interconnected in a certain way and thus forming an organised activity structure. The discussion of who does what and why has been undertaken without much consideration of dynamic aspects within such a context. However, in order to analyse change in activity structures the structures as such need to be described as a platform on which an understanding of the dynamics can be developed. It is important to consider the fact that activity structures are constantly both subject to and the cause of changes of different kinds. Each change that affects an activity structure in one way or another alters the conditions for subsequent changes.

One structural feature that affects the dynamics of activity structures is the principle of non-proportional change. This principle was formulated by Boulding (1953: 335) as: 'As any structure grows the proportions of its parts and of its significant variables cannot remain constant'. This problem thus refers to the first and second dimensions dealt with above and are effects of the 'imperfectly divisible factors' brought up by Teece (1980). Dixon and Wilkinson (1986: 38) also discuss a parallel problem which adds the third dimension:

> [T]he search for efficiency in the technical subsystem is constrained by problems of non-proportional growth in the administrative subsystem as the size of the firm increases and by the problem of matching the outputs of the firm to the requirements of the customers.

The technical subsystem may be seen as encompassing the first and second dimensions, while the administrative subsystem is attributable to the co-ordination of all activities of an individual firm, i.e., the third dimension. Hence, the reasons and effects of non-proportional growth are related to all three dimensions. However, this is but one of the structural features which lays the ground for the dynamics of activity structures since it touches only on *quantitative* aspects of *given* resources for *given* uses (activities). Therefore, when resources are not considered given either in terms of how they are combined or how they are activated (Penrose 1959; Håkansson 1993) structural aspects other than those concerned with non-proportional change are raised. These aspects are concerned with the structural prerequisites for finding new combinations and uses of resources.

Apart from structural factors, behavioural ones also need to be recognised. The efficiency of the activities performed by a supplier, directed towards one particular customer, is assumed to be dependent on the activities the supplier performs towards its other customers. If one of these customers chooses, for instance, to move a particular activity to the supplier (i.e., to add this activity to the ones already undertaken by the supplier), this may open up opportunities for other customers of the supplier. These firms may or may not choose to take advantage of these opportunities. However, the activity subject to movement is also related to other activities in the buying firm, and thereby to activities undertaken by third parties. A change by one firm may therefore call for various adjustments at several other firms. Moreover, some changes can be perceived as threats by some firms and/or as opportunities by others, regardless of potential efficiency gains. For instance, McGuiness (1991) argues that traditional models overestimate the role of efficiency. Since organisational change influences the distribution of power among economic actors, that power is not only exercised to achieve efficiency in economic terms. All this will naturally have consequences for the long-term effects of the changes, or, in other words, for the effectuation of subsequent changes.

Based on this framework, the division of individual activities among firms needs be analysed in the context of the activity structures they are part of. Such a context comprises highly complex structures which have to be delimited for different analytical purposes. One way to delimit an activity structure is to relate it to a particular end product. However, any end product related activity structure is also related to other such activity structures owing to horizontal interdependence. Therefore, as long as interdependence among activities prevails, it must be included if the analysis aims at increasing our understanding of change in activity structures.

Now the basic principles for the efficient organisation of activities among firms have been clarified, we may turn to reality, where we will gain insights into why the model is not easily applicable. Additional aspects of interdependence, complicating the matter further, are derived from the empirical illustrations. In the next chapter we return to the company having problems with how its activities might be organised, with which this book began. This empirical case, dealing with the company's efforts to reorganise its activities to obtain increased efficiency, is used as a basis for further exploration of the division of labour among firms.

Chapter 3

The SweFork case

CASE BACKGROUND

SweFork was founded in 1958. About forty years later its turnover is approximately one billion Swedish kronor and consists, apart from a parent company located in Sweden, of seven foreign subsidiaries. All development and manufacturing takes place at the Swedish site. The product range consists of a few basic truck models which are adapted to the end-users' requirements to different extents. A few thousand trucks per year are produced, the applications being loading, unloading, transporting, stacking and order picking. The production activities undertaken by SweFork are mainly welding, assembling and painting. The extent to which these and other production activities are undertaken by SweFork varies among the different truck models for different reasons, one of which is the fixed capacity of the welding and painting facilities.

About 3,000 different components of various sizes and values are purchased. Around 80 per cent of these items are subcontracted and are, hence, specific to SweFork's trucks. Over time the purchasing behaviour has been characterised by stability in terms of what has been purchased, while the way the suppliers have been dealt with has changed over the years. During quite a long initial period the suppliers were kept at arm's length. A low degree of dependency was preferred and was also a prerequisite for maintaining the sourcing situation, then characterised by multiple sourcing. For some reason, multiple sourcing was reduced in favour of single sourcing around the mid-1970s. Thereafter, relationships with the suppliers seem to have changed. Increasing dependence on individual suppliers has been a result of adjustments of different kinds from both sides of the buyer/seller relationships. In consequence, the occurrence of supplier changes has gone down. The adjustments have been of different kinds but are mainly related to time co-ordination and to quality enhancements. Delivery plans and quality contracts have been among the main tools in these efforts.

From component to system purchasing

During the late 1980s, discussions with SweFork's purchasing department concerning future development of purchasing raised a 'new' aspect of changed buying behaviour. Ideas about letting suppliers take on complete systems, instead of the company buying and then assembling separate components, were coming into focus. As a result, the component structure that had been almost entirely stable since the firm was founded was to be restructured. The previous stability in terms of what was bought was naturally related to other aspects of how the company operated at the time. For a long time, SweFork had used only about 3,000 components (n-details, e.g., screws and nuts excluded) while other similar firms (in terms of product range and production methods) used more than three times as many different components. This policy, referred to as the 'common component concept', was applied as a sales argument since it made service, stock-keeping and spare parts handling more efficient. Naturally, it also had an impact on other activities such as product development and purchasing.

The truck designs developed before the system purchasing policy was initiated were technically integrated (Figure 3.1.a shows the principle), meaning that the technical dependencies among the individual components were generally high. In order to be able to out-source entire systems, the designs had to be adapted. The objectives of the design changes were to keep technical dependencies among individual components within the systems, which may be interdependent on a system level (see Figure 3.1.b).

Therefore, a new truck under development was based on system thinking. The older truck models were to be developed as much as possible towards system design. However, for various reasons, most systems could only be implemented in the new truck model.

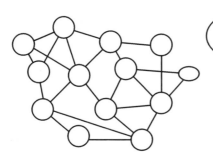 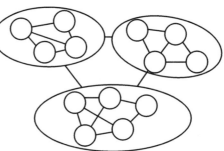

Figure 3.1.a Technical dependencies among components in integrated designs

Figure 3.1.b Technical dependencies among components in system designs

The new product

The new product, henceforth referred to as the T2–truck, was introduced on the market in April 1991 at the Hannover Messe Trade Fair. It was considered by the firm to be an entirely new product and not just a new model. The T2–truck was aimed at a new market segment consisting of stores and distributors which use these kinds of trucks for loading, lifting and short distance transportation. The T2–truck was the first truck developed by the firm manoeuvred by a walking driver, in contrast with the other trucks on which the driver stands or sits.

The T2–truck, which was to be the first model in a series of small trucks, was primarily developed for the European market, on which it is more common to have these kinds of trucks with walking drivers, in contrast with the trucks on the Swedish market. The total market for trucks of this type was estimated to about 45,000 units, the largest individual country market being Germany. During the first year of production about 500 units of the T2–truck were sold, which was lower than estimated but still fairly good considering the recession. The T2–truck received a great deal of attention from potential customers, and SweFork also received a design award for it.

Before the introduction of the new product, the plan was to produce 15 units, which would be sent out to subsidiaries and agents for test-driving and comments. However, owing to lack of time these tests could not be undertaken. 'Comments' from the users were therefore sent back to the company as claims, especially from French customers. One reason for their dissatisfaction was that the lifts were used differently than expected in some ways. For instance, the steering arm was used to sit on, which had not been considered during development. As a consequence, several design changes had to be made during the first year after introduction.

As mentioned above, one important condition during the development was that the new product should be built mainly using a set of systems bought from system suppliers responsible for assembly and inspection so the systems could go directly into SweFork's final assembly. Therefore, the in-house work (measured in terms of direct labour costs) on each unit, i.e., mainly final assembly, would be only about half of that needed for the other models. Another difference between this new product and the others was that the T2–truck was to be a standard product with just a few available options and produced to stock, in contrast to the other truck models produced by the company. These other truck models were based on a few basic model designs, but adapted to a large extent to end-customer specific requirements and produced on order. However, as it turned out, a large proportion of the T2–trucks were also adapted to the end-customers' requirements.

One year after the launch of the T2–truck the TP2–truck was introduced on the market. This version of the T2–truck, which was to replace an older model of one of the smallest trucks, has a platform mounted on it which also entailed other adaptations such as a shorter steering arm. Later, in 1992, an adapted version for cold stores was developed, which mainly included adaptations of the electrical parts in the truck.

The production system

The production manager at that time described the choice of production method as follows:

> The choice of method depends on the production volume. Various techniques are used to produce the different truck models. The production technique chosen for the T2–trucks means going back 7–8 years. Instead of having all components in the central supply store all material will now be kept in the work shop. The production costs per unit need to be reduced as volumes increase.

At first, a production method based on an assembly track, in which the assemblers walked from one assembly station to the next, adding systems and components in a sequence, was chosen (see Figure 3.2). However, this method turned out to be very sensitive to disturbances since the whole production process was stopped if one assembler had problems. An average of only 12–13 lifts per week could be produced, with a maximum of 15. The average production time per unit was 15 hours, but in the worst cases it could be up to 50 hours.

In order to achieve the planned production time, which was 12 hours, and also to be able to increase production to 30 and then to 40 units per week, production methods had to be changed. The increased production volume was partly due to the TP2 production. At this time, about 18 months after its introduction, production costs had not decreased as planned but had increased by 9 per cent compared with the costs one year earlier. The cost increase was assumed to be attributable to all the design changes that had been made. These were, in turn, mainly the result of problems in combining technical function and design. Another problem affecting production was that the truck contained a large number of moving parts, which were difficult to adjust to one another. Altogether it took an average of 90 minutes per unit to make adjustments after the different assembly steps. This was not included in the estimated assembly time. Therefore, a new production method was implemented, based on fixed work stations to which all parts that were to be assembled were brought (see Figure 3.3). Some components were pre-assembled into systems while others were assembled directly into what would be complete trucks. All systems and components were put into component sets which

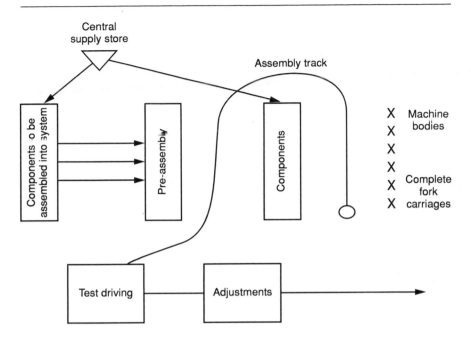

Figure 3.2 The first T2–truck production layout at SweFork

were brought to the fixed work stations. Handling the material in this way was considered more flexible in terms of disturbances and in terms of variations in production volumes.

Parallel to the implementation of this new production method other changes were made which impacted on the production system. One such change was that the flow of products in progress between assembly, welding and painting was altered and directed towards the needs in the final assembly station. The welding, painting and inspection units were general resources also used to produce other truck models. This resulted in some problems of fixed capacity and varying flows, since only the T2–trucks were produced continuously.

The only system that was out-sourced from the very beginning was the hydraulic system. For several reasons, the other systems were not out-sourced from the start but were initially pre-assembled in-house. One reason was that certain design changes were expected to be needed during the first year of production and that these 'teething troubles' were considered to be easier to solve with the assembly in-house. Another reason was that sales turned out to be lower than expected, owing to the recession, which meant for some of the systems that the actual volumes were too small for out-sourcing to be considered necessary or efficient.

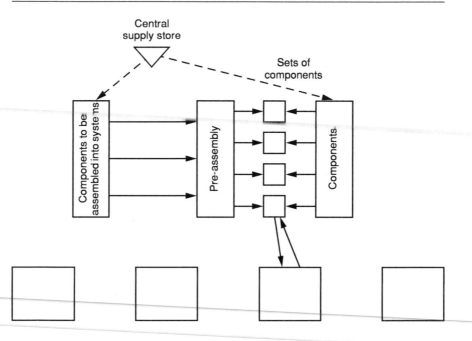

Figure 3.3 The second T2–truck production layout at SweFork

This was, in turn, partly a matter of excess capacity in the company's own work force. When the production goal was increased, the production department considered it urgent to out-source as many of the systems as possible. Those systems, including large numbers of components, came particularly into focus, since these were difficult to handle within the production system, to obtain efficient production flows.

Out-sourcing discussions within the company

In the late 1980s, SweFork, and especially the production function, was under great pressure, owing to booming sales. Shortage of production capacity was probably the most important reason why out-sourcing of systems came into focus. Another related reason may have been that large Swedish vehicle producers, such as Volvo Trucks and Scania, focused attention on the subject, which was not only noticed in the press, but also discussed by their common suppliers. Volvo's and Scania's suppliers were generally perceived as efficient in terms of production and as high quality producers.

SweFork's production manager at the time was considered to have quite a positive attitude towards out-sourcing of systems, although he was very much concerned that all decisions should be based on accurate cost estimates. However, the calculations were made using traditional product based accounting principles, implying that the added overheads were based partly on the value of the purchased items. Consequently, it was more or less impossible to achieve cost estimates in favour of buying. Another matter subject to discussions was control, such as how to deal with second tier suppliers and also what responsibilities should be out-sourced. Therefore, inspection and dependency matters became important issues subject to different opinions within the firm.

Calculation principles

The calculation principle applied was based on adding up the following:

- Production costs
- Production overheads (a certain percentage of the production costs)
- Materials costs
- Materials overheads (a certain percentage of the material costs).

This simplified accounting model, which until then had mainly been used to distribute the costs among the firm's products, was the basis for out-sourcing decisions. The production cost calculations were quite straightforward: the production time per item was multiplied by the cost per hour (which was quite equivalent for different Swedish suppliers). In other words, in order to reach a lower production cost the supplier had to be able to perform the production activities more efficiently than the customer. The main problems related to using this model when analysing whether a system should be out-sourced or assembled in-house concerned the materials overhead. Since this was added as a percentage of the value of the purchased material, i.e., the same percentage was added irrespective of whether several components or complete systems were bought (to which the suppliers added their own material overhead), it was very difficult, or impossible, to reach a system sourcing decision using this calculation model. Therefore, one question of concern for the purchasing department was: How should factors not included in the calculations be evaluated?

To obtain a more accurate picture of the costs for component versus system sourcing, one person working with internal logistics was assigned to make a thorough analysis of the actual cost differences. The costs associated with handling one item as compared with several was to be included in these estimates. For example, one of the potential system sourcing cases would result in the following benefits:

	In-house assembly	System sourcing
Number of units bought	10	1
Storage (value)	30	19
Storage space	10	1
Number of handlings, i.e., physical movements within the company	54	3

The person responsible for the analysis quit his job after a while and no one else took on the assignment. The existing accounting principles were then used as they were. The purchasers were frustrated over the fact that the estimates resulting from these calculation principles were not at all reflective of the actual costs. Apart from not considering the costs connected with activities that are supposed to be included in material overhead, adjustments needed after assembly (a total of 90 minutes per unit), and also costs connected with fulfilling guarantee engagements, were not included. All these inaccuracies made it look as though it would be less costly to produce in-house than to out-source.

Control aspects – second tier suppliers

Another issue that came into focus during the system sourcing discussions was anxiety about losing control of component suppliers who could become second tier suppliers owing to system sourcing. Three different alternative solutions to the problem were therefore discussed:

1 System suppliers buy components from suppliers specified by SweFork and on SweFork contracts.
2 SweFork specifies component suppliers but lets the system suppliers handle the purchases (including price negotiations).
3 System suppliers choose their own sources and make their own purchases.

Some purchasers felt there would be great risks associated with losing control over some of the second tier suppliers. One main argument was that the system suppliers would not be anxious enough, or able to keep prices down, which was assumed to lead to situations where the system suppliers just forwarded price increases from their own suppliers. SweFork had experienced such problems in a few cases in the past. Another important aspect of losing hold of second tier suppliers was losses in large volume purchases. This concerned all systems in which there were components that were also used in other trucks. For this reason, some of the system suppliers would be requested, according to the 'common component concept', to buy on SweFork's contracts, with apparent cost advantages but with consequences in terms of control, responsibilities and need for co-ordination. In some cases, the suppliers, however, had been found to buy even larger volumes of the components in question, or to get better price offers from their suppliers for other reasons. In a few such cases SweFork had even been offered the opportunity to buy on the suppliers' contracts.

However, other opinions were expressed. One of the purchasers argued that the only thing that would work in the long run would be to make the system suppliers fully responsible for their own purchases. Otherwise they would always blame the sub-suppliers, who had been forced upon them, for faults of various kinds as well as for price increases (in cases where the suppliers were specified and the system suppliers were handling the price negotiations). As a compromise, someone suggested that the system suppliers should be free to buy from whatever suppliers they choose, but that they should be obliged to render account for all their sources, which would allow SweFork to check and compare prices if necessary. Furthermore, this could give SweFork access to new and better component and material suppliers when collaborating with the system suppliers. In other cases the system supplier might have access to better sources if both parties accounted for their suppliers openly. For example, someone mentioned one system supplier who got a supplier from SweFork whom they could also use for production directed towards other customers.

What responsibilities should be out-sourced?

Control issues like those described above were the underlying issues determining what responsibilities would be out-sourced. The main activities concerned were component purchasing, assembly and design. A wide spectrum of alternatives ranged from traditional subcontracting of system assembly based on drawings, detailed work instructions and components bought according to SweFork's contracts, to system suppliers fully responsible for their sourcing, assembly and design (specified in relation to the function of the system in terms of performance and outer dimensions).

Supplier involvement in development and design was a fundamental issue. Letting the suppliers become fully responsible, i.e., even for designing the systems, was considered necessary by some purchasers. One purchaser said: 'The system suppliers must become involved to a greater extent, otherwise they cannot be made fully responsible for the production of the systems.' According to this purchaser, subcontractors had became involved too late in the development process, which resulted in their having no actual influence on the design. This made it impossible for them to be efficient in their production activities.

The design department was considered to have a rather conservative attitude towards out-sourcing design responsibilities although they had begun, increasingly, to consult the suppliers to suggest alternative design solutions. However, this interaction with the suppliers was often initiated too late in the process for the suppliers to have any actual impact, and since most major changes called for subsequent adjustments of different kinds, affecting both SweFork's internal activities and other suppliers' activities, their suggestions were often considered difficult to take into account. One reason suggested for the design department's conservative attitudes was concern about control – 'it is complex enough as it is' – rather than fear of staff cutbacks.

One SweFork purchaser said that from a strictly cost point of view it would probably be efficient to out-source several systems, but that the organisation was not yet 'mature' enough to handle it, although he thought the prerequisites were improving. In recent years the possibilities of recognising the opportunities in system sourcing – or out-sourcing of whole technical functions – had improved. Apprehensions were related to the current situation in which there was a high degree of value added outside the company and the fact that almost everything was still designed in-house and therefore controlled by SweFork. The reason for these apprehensions was that the design personnel were too far away from where the production was located and were thus unable to stay in touch with developments, for instance of new production methods and new materials. Every now and then suppliers spontaneously called to ask why such obsolete production methods and/or materials had been chosen. These suppliers also sometimes suggested other solutions, which were often rejected because of additional needs for adjustments within other parts of the truck and/or SweFork's production. There was also sometimes a rather suspicious attitude towards proposed changes resulting in perceived advantages for the suppliers.

Some systems of interest had also been developed or were currently being developed by firms whose customers were putting pressure on them to integrate more or less standardised systems. Hence, the question that arose concerning these systems tended to be whether to join the on-going development. 'Is it possible to stay outside?' was considered to be an important question. One apparent benefit, apart from direct cost savings in buying systems produced in larger volumes, was that participation could make it possible to gain some influence on the on-going development.

Inspection

Inspection matters also came into focus as a consequence of the out-sourcing discussions. It was difficult to set the terms for some critical activities in work instructions, especially those related to learning from experience. These activities could not be described exactly and were therefore perceived as potential sources of conflict in an out-sourcing situation, although the problems would be similar if handled within the organisation. This was also the main reason why SweFork initially chose to undertake most pre-assembly activities (of components into systems) in-house instead of having them out-sourced from the start of production.

Certain faults were discovered in production. These could either have been attributable to incorrect components or to mistakes made in production. Regardless of the reasons, they were often corrected in-house. When faults were discovered by the users of the end-products they resulted in claims. However, claims follow-up had not been working very well, and routines for handling them were discussed. For this reason, the costs for guarantee fulfilments as well as the sources of these costs were difficult to identify and assess.

The potential system suppliers who had been involved in system sourcing discussions were also concerned about how inspection matters should be handled if they were going to be responsible for the purchasing of components, especially if they were, or wanted to become, certified ISO 9000 suppliers. If they were not going to buy components on the customers' contracts they would become responsible for all parts included in the systems they supplied. Another important inspection matter was that in some of the systems subjected to out-sourcing discussions, there were difficulties in discovering certain faults at a particular stage of assembly without special testing equipment. Additional investments would therefore probably be needed.

Becoming dependent

Dependency issues were considered difficult to handle. Fear of becoming dependent on system suppliers was in the background of the discussions, without being addressed directly. Welding jobs that had previously been out-sourced owing to capacity variations had not resulted in any difficult dependency situations since the capabilities had remained within the firm. The concerns regarding the welding contractors were quite the opposite – some of these were small firms which were considered too dependent on SweFork.

Seen in a long-term perspective, dependencies had been handled in different ways over the years. First, multiple sourcing was one common way of keeping dependency on individual suppliers low. Later, when the advantages of single sourcing were recognised, dependencies were handled by staying informed of alternative suppliers. Although supplier switching costs were considered high, it was still possible to change suppliers if necessary, and this was occasionally also done. However, increasing the specificity of what was bought also meant reducing the possibilities of making quick supplier changes since there would be no immediate alternative sources, at least not in a short-term perspective. One way of reducing the degree of dependency on individual suppliers had been, whenever possible, to own all specific tools used by suppliers, although this had meant that some potential suppliers who wanted partial ownership of the tools had not been interested in becoming suppliers under these conditions.

THE SYSTEMS SUBJECT TO OUT-SOURCING

A total of 6–8 systems within the T2–truck were the subject of out-sourcing discussions. Four system cases are presented in the following sections: the hydraulic system, the steering arm, the complete fork carriage and the machine body. The systems differ from one another in several ways. Some of these differences are dealt with below as they have affected the way the cases are described and discussed.

The hydraulic system belonging to the T2–truck was the only system that was out-sourced from the start, i.e., when the production of the T2–trucks begun. Hence, the emphasis in this case was on the activity structure of which SweFork became a part, by out-sourcing the hydraulic system to a particular system supplier. Therefore, the system supplier and its suppliers and customers are in focus in this case.

Owing to various problems and technical complexities the steering arm was not out-sourced from the start, although the intention was to out-source the system when the problems had been solved. However, as it turned out only one small part of this system (the handles) was actually out-sourced, owing to changing conditions in general and interdependence created in the process. Therefore, some aspects relating to the out-sourcing process are dealt with in this case as these impacted on the structural prerequisites for out-sourcing this system.

The complete fork carriages were not out-sourced during the period studied, as intended by SweFork. Therefore, the activity structure of which the potential system supplier was a part is focused on in this case, as it could have been used if the complete fork carriage had been out-sourced to this supplier.

The fourth and final system described is the machine body. Although this system was not a part of the T2–truck, the conditions were similar. The machine body was first made in-house by SweFork and later out-sourced to a system supplier. However, owing to the recession, the machine body was partly in-sourced again a few years later. The way the activities were organised during these three phases is therefore focused on in this case, as well as the interdependence created in the process.

The structure of the case presentations and discussions is not intended to enable comparison among the cases. Instead, the aim is to use the cases as illustrations of *different* conditions for changes of the division of work among firms and, as such, to let them contribute their different aspects of relevance.

The hydraulic system

The only system out-sourced from the very start was the hydraulic system. This system consisted of one main component – the hydraulic unit – a standardised system containing an electric motor, a pump and a tank. Additional components such as hoses, connections, brackets, rubber dampings and n-details were needed to mount the hydraulic unit to the truck.

The cost estimates made by SweFork showed a rather small cost difference – only about 2 per cent of the total cost for the whole system – in favour of undertaking the assembly of the hydraulic systems in-house. The labour time required to assemble the systems in-house was estimated to be about 14 minutes per item. Yet the hydraulic system was still out-sourced, for several reasons. When the out-sourcing decision was taken, the hydraulic system was considered easy to overview economically as well as technically. It was also perceived as easy to administer the out-sourcing of it since, compared with other systems, it had relatively few parts. This, in turn, was mainly a consequence of having chosen the hydraulic unit at an early stage during development of the T2–truck. In addition, out-sourcing the assembly of the hydraulic systems meant that the complete hydraulic systems could be sent directly into SweFork's final assembly.

This type of hydraulic system could only be used in the T2–trucks. The larger truck models were not designed in favour of system assembly and the hydraulic components were technically integrated into other parts of the truck. Consequently, no similar integrated hydraulic units were used in other trucks. Instead, all the individual components were purchased and mounted separately. However, some of the additional components needed to connect the hydraulics with other parts of the T2–truck were similar to those used in other truck models. Moreover, if the system supplier was to be responsible for purchasing these additional components from its own sources, certain minor design changes would be required, which also affected other parts of the truck. For these reasons, SweFork required that the additional components should be bought from its own suppliers, and even on its contracts, when the hydraulic system was out-sourced. In order for the system supplier to be made responsible for these purchases, quite substantial price differences would be required for SweFork to accept such an offer.

HP – the supplier of hydraulic systems

HP, a small firm located in the south of Sweden, was founded in 1985, and its turnover in 1993 was about SEK 14 million. Among HP's ten suppliers a French producer of the hydraulic units was dominant. More

than half of HP's purchasing volume was bought from this supplier. HP
was the Swedish agent for this company and the agreement had been
extended to include the other Nordic markets. However, sales outside
Sweden only accounted for about 5 per cent of HP's sales. Outside France,
HP was the French supplier's second largest sales organisation in Europe
after the German agent, although only 2 per cent of the French supplier's
sales went through HP. Apart from this dominant supplier, HP had also
developed close relationships with a few suppliers of additional components. Some of these components were standardised while others were
customer specific (i.e., specific to HP's customers). Furthermore, some of
the standardised components were bought from distributors. Together, the
five largest suppliers accounted for about 90 per cent of HP's purchasing
volume.

The customer structure was less concentrated. The five largest customers
accounted for less than one-third of the sales, and about 20 customers
bought for more than SEK 100,000 annually. Together there were more
than 800 customers in the customer file, but not all of them bought on a
regular basis. In Figure 3.4 the five largest suppliers and customers are
shown. The different sizes of the firms are illustrated as well as the sizes
of the flows to and from HP.

HP's role 'in the middle'

There were large differences among the customers and suppliers in terms
of size and end-products. Despite this, and although the relative importance of the relationships with HP differed among them, there were also
interesting similarities in how the customers and suppliers related to HP.

Production

The suppliers all produced or distributed components produced in batches,
and all customers primarily assembled parts into equipment. HP's role
between the suppliers and customers was to gather and assemble components complementary to the main hydraulic unit into customer specific
systems. Among the five most important suppliers, two (nos. 2 and 5)
produced customer specific components from raw materials, while the
others manufactured or distributed standard components. In two cases,
HP used parallel suppliers. One of them was a small Danish producer of
customer specific components (supplier 2 in Figure 3.4). This supplier
designed and manufactured very important components for HP. The
designs were specific to each of HP's customers and the supplier had the
ownership rights to the designs and prototypes. The supplier's general
manager was considered a key person since the daily operations were very
much dependent upon him. When he suddenly had an accident, HP's

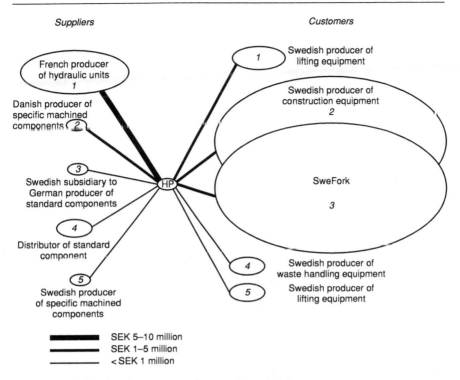

Figure 3.4 HP's five largest suppliers and customers

vulnerability and dependence on the Danish supplier became painfully clear. As a result, an additional supplier (supplier 5) was found and thereafter supplied 10 per cent of the purchased volume of this component. However, both these suppliers required certain minimum production volumes to be interested in making customer specific solutions, which made this dual sourcing situation a delicate balance issue for HP. In the second case, a parallel supplier was used from time to time when some of the customers (or their customers) required a particular brand of a standardised component.

Compared with what was done both by most of its suppliers and customers, the value added by HP was rather small. The assembly activities took between 5 and 10 minutes per system. If additional activities such as internal logistics were incorporated, the direct labour time added to each unit still seldom exceeded 20 minutes. Thus, in relation to the total cost for each system, the share of the costs for the activities done by HP was marginal. For example, less than 2 per cent of the value of the hydraulic systems sold to SweFork was related to the assembly activity undertaken by HP.

HP's sales had been fluctuating. In the early 1990s sales fell owing to the recession. The demand for the equipment produced by HP's customers was very sensitive to variations in the general economic climate. However, a few years later sales went up noticeably, mainly due to increased commitments vis-à-vis HP's current customers. The scope of what was bought in terms both of the numbers of components within each customer specific system, as well as in terms of the assembly activities performed by HP, had increased. This could be interpreted as HP strengthening its position between suppliers and customers, making the firm more difficult to replace. Two additional factors contributed to this. One was that none of the important suppliers (in terms of value as well as in technical function) were suppliers to HP's competitors. Therefore, to get access, especially to the hydraulic units produced by the French firm, HP had to be used as the supplier, as it was the only available source in Sweden. The other factor was that the supplier switching costs were high since supplier changes, among other things, required that design changes had to be made by the customers. SweFork was the only one of the five customers in focus who also bought from HP's competitors, although not complete systems, and used them within other product models than the one supplied to by HP. Moreover, the French hydraulic unit supplier had developed more powerful units that could contribute to increasing the performance of the customers' end products. HP's customers had begun to focus attention on these new units, and this was expected to impact positively on HP's future sales. SweFork was among the first customers to choose these new units for the T2–trucks.

Changes in HP's own activities were very much affected by the counterparts, since they were focused on quality matters. Two of the suppliers (nos. 1 and 3) were certified by the ISO 9000 standard, which meant that HP did not need to inspect these components until after they had been mounted together with other parts. Two other suppliers (nos. 4 and 5) were, like HP, currently working on being certified. This meant that in the future HP would have less need to inspect incoming components, while it would have to put more efforts into the inspection of assembled systems.

Product development

HP's role in terms of product development was quite small. For one thing, HP brought the dominant supplier of hydraulic units and the customers together when the customers developed new or modified products. The supplier had been developing general technical abilities through close collaboration with demanding customers in the French defence and automobile industries. This had forced the supplier to cope with high quality demands and to develop standard hydraulic units that permitted customer specific adjustments to be made. Hence the hydraulic unit supplier did not develop customer specific solutions, but made rather simple adjustments of flows and pressures within its standard units to suit each customer's needs. However, seen from the customers' point of view, this could be an important part in the development of new or modified products since the hydraulic unit's performance affected the overall performance of the equipment produced. It also affected, for example, what dimensions could be set on certain parts in it. Therefore, HP arranged and participated in meetings between the French supplier and the customers when the customers were developing new products. Apart from organising and participating in such meetings, HP also designed the systems, i.e., the composition of the additional parts that complemented the hydraulic unit. This was mainly a question of choosing the right standard components and of designing, or letting the customer specific component suppliers design, additional parts.

The above concerns what we may call system customers, a category to which all five of the most important customers belonged. However, another customer category, which may be referred to as standard component customers, was also handled by HP. Vis-à-vis this latter category HP could be described as quite a traditional distributor since the adjustments, if any, were made in terms of how the exchange was handled, while *what* was exchanged was standardised.

Relationships between HP and its counterparts

Seven of the ten relationships were established at the time HP was founded. The owner already knew most of these firms since he had previously worked in the same technical area for other firms. Hence, the social part of the relationships, in several cases, was much longer than eight years. The only supplier relationship (no. 5) which was of more recent date was established when a parallel source to supplier 2 had to be found (see above). The two 'new' customer relationships (no. 2 and SweFork) were established in the early 1990s, although discussions of a technical and commercial nature began a few years earlier.

With eight of the ten counterparts, the degree of formalisation concerning the agreements was low. Ordinary buying agreements that could be broken at any time were applied. The interdependence was thus related to the technical ties between the parties. Since the system customers had to make design changes in their products if they replaced HP with another supplier, these ties were more difficult to break. Two of the supplier agreements (nos. 1 and 3) were of another nature. The agent agreement with the French supplier has already been mentioned, but HP also had an exclusive agreement with supplier 3. The agreement included the right to sell a limited range of this supplier's products in southern Sweden.

Table 3.1   Connections between HP's suppliers and customers

		Supplier				
		1	2	3	4	5
Customer	1	a, c	c	c		c
	2	a, b, c	c			
	3 (SweFork)	a, c				
	4	a, c	c			
	5	a, c	c	c		c

Connections between HP's suppliers and customers

Three kinds of connections between the suppliers and the customers could be found. First, there were direct contacts, co-ordinated by HP, concerning development issues as described above (marked 'a' in Table 3.1). Secondly, in one case, there were direct deliveries from one supplier to one of the customers (marked 'b' in the table) which were administrated by HP. Thirdly, there were connections between the suppliers and the customers in terms of what components were incorporated into the systems assembled and supplied by HP (marked 'c' in the table).

One clear observation regarding Table 3.1 is the concentration on the French supplier, which also concerned many other customers than these five most important ones. For SweFork, the additional components that were mounted into their systems were all bought from SweFork's own suppliers. As mentioned, this was because SweFork bought these components for other purposes, and also because they were afraid of losing control over these suppliers.

Analysis of the activity structure

The activities undertaken by HP and its suppliers in relation to the different system customers were similar in some respects. As a starting point for discussion, these activities can be exemplified by the activities directed to customer 1 (see Figure 3.4 and Table 3.1), shown in Figure 3.5.

Figure 3.5 shows how the specific part of the activity structure resulting in the hydraulic systems designed to suit customer 1's end products had its starting point at different locations. Prior to the start of every specific activity chain (ending in customer 1's end product) there was a general activity that could also be directed to other customers, i.e., the result of the activity could be used in other customers' end products. For instance, the specific component produced by supplier 2 could not be put into another customer's system, but because the materials used in the process were general, they could be machined by the supplier to suit other customers' needs. Moreover, the resources activated by suppliers in the

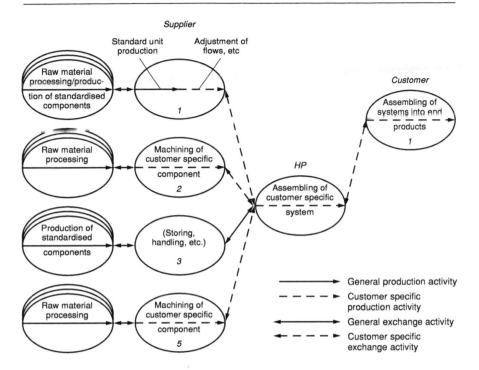

Figure 3.5 An example of a part of an end product related activity structure

production of the specific components as well as HP's own resources used in the assembly activities undertaken could also be used for all system customers.

The reason using HP could be regarded as an efficient solution by the system customers was not primarily related to the customers' inabilities to perform the assembly activities undertaken by HP, but rather for the individual system customer to efficiently co-ordinate the whole bundle of activities needed. The reason HP was better suited to doing this than the individual customers may be related to the fact that there were similarities in the different customers' needs, and that various economies of scale could be taken advantage of. Thus, although every system customer was given unique solutions to suit their own end products (although standard components were included in their systems) the supplier relationships developed by HP could be regarded as a resource they could utilise on a larger scale than that of any individual customer. The relationships between HP and the system customers varied in complexity, but in one important respect – the degree and nature of customer specific activities developed – there were consistent similarities in terms of the customers' needs as related to the different suppliers. For example, the Danish producer of specific machined components (supplier 2) designed the components in co-operation with HP, who knew what parts this component would be connected to. All designs made by the Danish supplier were different, but the activities were similar in terms of raw material and machining equipment used. Thus, the resources activated to produce the customer specific components could be shared among the system customers. The resulting economies of scale can be related both to the use of tangible resources such as raw materials and equipment, as well as to intangible resources such as HP's knowledge about the resources and activities controlled by the supplier. The activity chains directed to HP's different system customers were therefore not only connected to one another by the assembling activities undertaken by HP in which the personnel and equipment activated could be shared, but also by some of HP's suppliers' (the producers of specific components) activities.

The efforts made to improve the quality of the products exchanged among the firms involved, mainly by emphasising inspection of the results of each firm's production activities (instead of having all of them inspecting purchased components at arrival), increased the benefits derived from similarities among the customers' needs. This could be achieved because of the results of each firm's activities being more similar than the various products bought by their customers (making inspection of purchased products less similar). Obviously it was also more efficient, since faults could be corrected by the firm that discovered them.

Most of HP's supplier relationships could as activated resources be shared among the customers, who thereby could benefit from similarities among their needs in terms of knowledge and activity co-ordination. The co-ordination of activities could both be related to the sequentially dependent activities within the activity chains directed towards the different customers, and to the co-ordination among these chains. Also, general large-scale purchasing benefits, such as lower prices and less transportation and administration, could be achieved, making the costs incurred in handling each supplier relationship lower (as a share of the purchase value) compared with what any individual customer could obtain. These general large-scale purchasing benefits could be achieved both in terms of standardised and specific components, and were also relevant to both the system customers and the standard component customers who used HP as a distributor.

Furthermore, there was volume interdependence between the activities undertaken by two of the suppliers who were not willing to make specific components if the (aggregated) production volumes were not large enough. This volume interdependence could be handled by HP through co-ordination of the customers' need for these components, although the individual customers did not require large enough volumes to be able to use these suppliers.

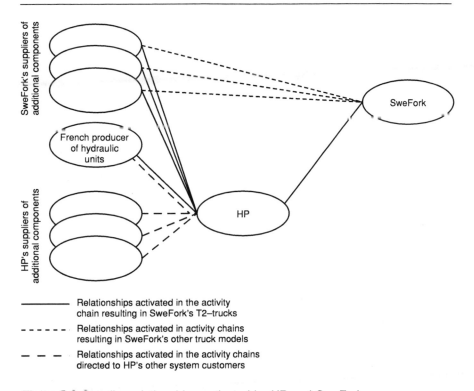

Relationships activated in the activity
chain resulting in SweFork's T2–trucks

Relationships activated in activity chains
resulting in SweFork's other truck models

Relationships activated in the activity chains
directed to HP's other system customers

Figure 3.6 Supplier relationships activated by HP and SweFork

The activity chains resulting in SweFork's hydraulic systems, as compared with the other system customers, were not as closely connected to the other activity chains handled by HP. Connections to the other chains existed in the assembly undertaken by HP, and in the activities undertaken by the French hydraulic unit producer, but SweFork chose not to use HP's suppliers of the additional components needed in the hydraulic systems. These chains were therefore connected to SweFork's other activity chains instead, resulting in the larger trucks produced by SweFork. The situation is illustrated in Figure 3.6 showing the relationships that were activated.

As regards the additional components, SweFork chose to take advantage of similarities among activity chains resulting in its different truck models instead of exploiting those created by HP. One reason for this was that there was interdependence among these and certain other activities within SweFork such as spare parts handling and service. From SweFork's point of view this was considered an efficient way of organising the activities.

Summary

This case illustrates how parts of different firms' end product related activity structures can be interconnected. Clear efficiency gains were achieved through economising on similarities in the different customers' needs satisfied by the system supplier. By co-ordinating the activities vertically into activity chains directed towards the different customers, and by connecting the activities incorporated in the different activity chains horizontally (i.e., making them share common resources), the supplier was able to supply all system customers with hydraulic systems specifically adapted to the customers' end products, and also to organise the activity structure more efficiently than any individual customer would have been able to do. '

The steering arm

The steering arm consisted mainly of two parts: the handle, containing about ten different components, and the speed control, with about twenty components. Apart from these two part-systems, there were about five additional components in the steering arm, so that altogether there were some 35 different components in the system. All these components were bought from suppliers. The steering arm was characterised by its relatively large number of components with comparably low purchase values. Moreover, especially in the speed control, there were several moving parts that had to fit exactly in order for the steering arm to function. Some of the components in the steering arm were plastic, made by injection moulding. SweFork had no previous experience either of the material or of the production technique, since the steering arms used in the other truck models were very different in terms of design and materials. Injection moulded plastic components were chosen for design reasons, and were also considered cost efficient because of the comparably large volumes of T2–trucks that were going to be produced. The tools necessary for the injection moulding technique require investments, but if the volumes are large enough the cost per item is very low.

Pre-assembly of the steering arm was first undertaken in-house by SweFork, mainly because there were many teething troubles to be solved before the system could be considered ready to be out-sourced. The problems were many, mainly related to difficulties in assembly, and to insufficient strength of some of the components. The problems caused by insufficient strength concerned the injection moulded plastic components and were explained by SweFork's lack of previous experience. Assembly was complicated because of all the moving parts that had to be inter-adjusted. As it turned out, the adjustments needed after the actual assembly required almost as much time as the assembly itself. As a consequence of these problems, many minor design changes were made – about 50 such changes were made during the first year of production. Most of these changes also affected other components in the system, directly and indirectly. Furthermore, certain components were more difficult to change than others because specific tools were used in their production. In some instances, these tools were adjustable in some dimensions, but not in others. Hence, some of the changes required that the tools be replaced, which was costly, time consuming and also required extensive co-ordination among all parties involved. The latter was required not only because the components produced by the suppliers were changed, but also because SweFork needed access to the suppliers' knowledge. Afterwards, someone at SweFork said that the suppliers should have been more involved, and earlier. For instance, some of the suppliers could have been used as advisors concerning choices of standard components.

Apart from the general motivation for out-sourcing, the steering arm was given high priority because of all the problems experienced in assembly. The assembly was undertaken in the pre-assembly workshop at SweFork, and was considered to be very different from other pre-assembly operations. Generally, the degree of similarity among the pre-assembled systems was low. The assembly of the steering arm was divided into three parts. First the handle and the speed control were assembled separately and thereafter they were mounted together along with the five additional components. The time required to assemble the handle was estimated at 5 minutes, and the speed control at 15 minutes (not including the adjustments needed after assembly). The last assembly step required 55 minutes. The main activities are shown in Figure 3.7.

Hence, the whole steering arm was characterised not only by a low purchase value, but also by relatively high direct labour costs. Because of the calculation principles applied (see p. 43–44), this caused problems

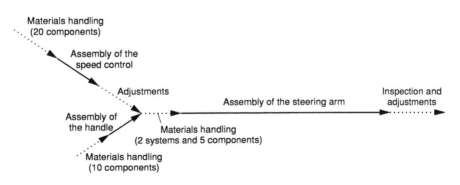

Figure 3.7 Main activities needed from purchasing of components until steering arm could be sent into final assembly

when the steering arm was to be out-sourced. The material overhead, which was added as a percentage of the direct material cost, was fairly low, while the actual activities associated with it (purchasing and materials handling) were extensive. However, the extensive adjustments needed after assembly were not incorporated in the calculations but were rather to be included in the production overhead. Despite these calculations resulting in cost estimates considered to be lower than the real costs, one of the potential system assemblers tendered a price just below the calculated costs on the two part-systems (although on a rather vague basis). The last step of the assembly, and the most time consuming one, was not calculated as cost efficient to out-source. The out-sourcing discussions were on-going at the same time as design changes were made, resulting in changing conditions for what was to be out-sourced. When SweFork and the system supplier were to come to an agreement, which was about two years after the start of production, only the handles were actually out-sourced, for several reasons. First, the speed control was still very complex to assemble and adjust. The adjustments were also subject to learning from experience, which made it difficult for SweFork to specify the detailed work instructions required by the system supplier. Secondly, the recession had begun to affect SweFork, with a severe reduction in demand, which made them generally less motivated to out-source. Thirdly, although many design changes had been made to solve the assembly problems and some problems relating to the strength of certain components, it was decided that the steering arm, and especially the speed control, should be entirely revised, and therefore there was no point in out-sourcing the whole system yet.

The system supplier – Industrial Plastics

Several of the component suppliers were at first considered potential system suppliers since they were actively seeking opportunities to refine the components they produced. Later, only two of them were actually asked for quotations. The system supplier chosen to take on the assembly of the handles, henceforth referred to as Industrial Plastics, was an injection moulding firm that supplied most of the plastic components. This relationship was fairly new, as it was established when the T2–truck was developed.

Apart from striving for increased added value, Industrial Plastics, which considered itself heavily dependent on one large customer, was striving to reduce this dependence by developing the relationships with its smaller customers. Therefore, although SweFork was not a large customer in terms of purchase value, Industrial Plastics considered it important because of the opportunities that could be developed by using SweFork, especially the assembly operation undertaken, as a future reference.

Industrial Plastics' customers had a few general requirements in common but, apart from this, they were different. Delivery reliability was considered important by most of the customers since they were using the plastic components in their end products. IT-based communication systems and standards such as Odette were applied and used in communication with a few of the major customers. Moreover, a growing share of Industrial Plastics' customers were, or were trying to become, certified ISO 9000 suppliers. Apart from these rather general requirements concerning just-in-time deliveries and quality, the customers were different in terms of what kinds of products they manufactured as well as in terms of their production activities.

All in all, Industrial Plastics had about ninety customers. The most important customer, a producer of electrical domestic appliances, alone accounted for about 20 per cent of the turnover. Industrial Plastics produced plastic components for this customer which were refined, mainly with printing. For another major customer, a producer of manual tools, Industrial Plastics made the whole end product including assembly of components. Some of these components were produced in-house and some were purchased from other firms. This means that Industrial Plastics contributed to its customers' end products to varying extents from production of single components to entire end products sold by the customers.

Production

The production activities undertaken by Industrial Plastics mainly had two parts: injection moulding of plastic parts, and refinements. In a third part of the factory, tool maintenance and repair were undertaken. The basis for Industrial Plastics' whole operation was injection moulding, for which several machines were used. The machines, some of which were served by robots, and the personnel handling them, could be considered as general resources (i.e., resources that could be used for all customers), while the tools used in the machines were specific to each customer. Various plastic raw materials could be used in the machines (depending on temperatures, etc.) to give the components produced in them their required characteristics.

Although the tools, which in most cases were owned by the customers, were sometimes considered expensive by the customers, these costs were fairly low compared with the costs for the machines and the personnel.

The injection moulded components could be refined by Industrial Plastics through various activities. Mainly, different kinds of printing on the components such as signs on buttons, as well as painting, ultra-sound welding and foliation, were done. In addition, some minor assembly operations were done for a few of the customers. All these refining activities were performed in a separate workshop in which eleven of the approximately forty employees worked. Among the refining activities Industrial Plastics wanted to expand was assembly. One reason for this was that system sourcing had received attention among several of Industrial Plastics' major customers and was considered both an opportunity and a potential threat, as Industrial Plastics disliked the idea of becoming a second tier supplier.

Taking on the assembly of the handles would impact in different ways on Industrial Plastics' activities. What purchasing responsibilities should be left to the system supplier was not discussed much, but three aspects were brought up. First, Industrial Plastics wanted to take on some additional components in its own production to enhance its capacity utilisation in the injection moulding. Secondly, the efforts made to become ISO 9000 certified imposed certain important requirements on the components not to be produced by Industrial Plastics. If the components were sent by SweFork they would not have to be inspected according to the ISO standard as Industrial Plastics would not be responsible for their quality, whereas if they were responsible for purchasing of components, Industrial Plastics would also be responsible for their quality. Thirdly, Industrial Plastics had a few relationships with component suppliers they would like to use instead of some of SweFork's suppliers.

In terms of refinements, the assembly would be added. Although Industrial Plastics had very little experience of assembly, it was considered by SweFork to be creative in developing assembly fixtures made in the tool maintenance workshop. However, Industrial Plastics considered the assembly of the handles to be complex compared with its past assembly experience.

Development

In order to be able to develop and manufacture the customer specific tools used in the injection moulding, Industrial Plastics had developed a few important relationships with other firms specialising in tool development and production. The most important of these was with a plastics consultancy bureau which had design competence Industrial Plastics considered useful. Moreover, four tool manufacturers were used from time to time. One of them was situated in Thailand, and was used to develop SweFork's tools. In SweFork's view, the tool production was more costly and required longer time than expected. In Industrial Plastics' view, this was a consequence of the fact that the design of the components was subject to changes during the development process.

Later, when the original tools were ready and production had begun, improvement of the strength of some of the plastic components was needed. The capacity of the injection moulding machines in terms, for instance, of what pressures could be obtained in combination with the plastic raw material used, determined how the tools, and thus the components, could be designed. Two alternatives were considered for solving the problems caused by insufficient strength: either the tool or the choice of material could be altered. Changing the tools was generally costly and, furthermore, impacted on directly and indirectly connected components which consequently had to be redesigned. The best choice was considered to be another material which was stronger but also more expensive. Neither the tools nor any connected components would be affected by such a change.

Other components and suppliers involved

The component and supplier structures were complicated in this case because of the large numbers of components and suppliers involved. Moreover, the fact that SweFork had no previous experience either of injection moulding techniques or of the plastic material used complicated the situation further.

The components and the suppliers involved in the steering arm can be categorised in different ways. First, more than half of the components were specific to the steering arm belonging to the T2–truck, while the rest were standardised components. Secondly, a few of the standardised components were also used in other truck models but not to a large extent, since the steering arm in the T2–truck was very different from the steering arms used in the other truck models. Thirdly, some of the components were bought from suppliers with whom SweFork had developed relationships that were considered very important. From these suppliers, various other components used in different truck models were purchased. Consequently, SweFork wanted to maintain these relationships and would therefore not let any system supplier take on these purchases or even let them negotiate on their own. The different supplier categories and their respective connections to SweFork's truck production are shown in Figure 3.8.

The design changes affected the components which required involvement of the suppliers producing them to different extents. When a change of a specific component was made, the supplier was usually involved. When a change affected a tool used by a supplier, even the supplier's tool supplier had to be involved in the change. On one occasion, a specific component was replaced by a standardised component, which also resulted in a change of supplier.

The costs per item of some of the specific components that were produced without specific tools could be reduced if tools were developed. These decisions affected the cost structure and depended on what volumes could be expected in the future. However, as long as design changes were still frequently made, most of the components that did not absolutely require tools were produced without them, and these decisions had to be made later.

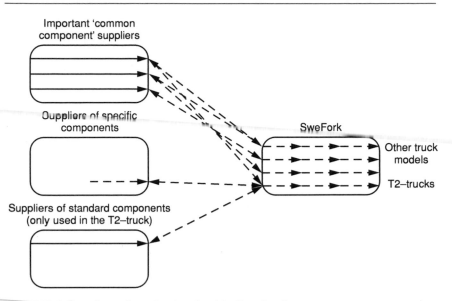

Figure 3.8 Supplier categories involved in the steering arm

Some suppliers of specific components were having quality problems and were therefore engaged in quality projects initiated by SweFork. The problems were complicated, since faulty components were not identified until the whole steering arm was completely assembled and could be tested as such. The faults were therefore very costly, since they were discovered late in the activity chain. In some instances these problems could be solved by investments in inspection equipment for use by some of the suppliers.

Owing to the low value of many of the specific components, in order to obtain cost efficiency, they were produced in batches large enough to cover one year's need of those components and, consequently, delivered only once per year. This also caused difficulties in bringing about the design changes needed.

Analysis of the activity structure

The situation surrounding the out-sourcing of the steering arm was obviously quite complex, not least because of the large numbers of components and suppliers involved. We begin by analysing the activity structure and the actual and potential changes concerning the main activities, before dealing with the complicated supplier structure and the required co-ordination of the suppliers' activities.

The injection moulding already undertaken by Industrial Plastics seemed to be characterised by a high degree of similarity since a large extent of the activated resources could be shared among other customers to Industrial Plastics. For the refining activities undertaken by Industrial Plastics, the degree of similarity seemed to be much lower. Various different activities were undertaken at the refining workshop. The activities and the resources activated varied in terms of sharing among the activity chains directed towards the different customers. Printing, for example, was performed for several customers while at that time assembly was not undertaken for more than a few customers. The degree of similarity among the assembling operations directed towards SweFork and refining activities directed towards other customers was low. Furthermore, Industrial Plastics considered the assembly of the handles more complicated than other assembly in its past experience. Even so, Industrial Plastics had the ambition of developing its assembly capabilities by finding additional customers with needs similar to those of SweFork. This would then increase the opportunities to enhance efficiency on this kind of assembly, since their skills, in terms of learning from experience, could be improved.

At the time when the out-sourcing was decided on, neither SweFork nor Industrial Plastics could benefit from any real similarities in the assembly of the two part-systems and other assembly activities undertaken by them. Hence they could be considered equally (in)efficient in terms of these activities. However, if Industrial Plastics were to succeed in their efforts to get additional assembling activities similar to the ones undertaken for SweFork, they could potentially become more efficient than SweFork. SweFork would probably not be developing any other systems similar to this one in the future. Furthermore, the assembly time required to produce one year's supply of handles was just about 100 hours. It would, therefore, have been difficult for SweFork to gain any learning effects in-house.

In this case, the activities related to purchasing, including supplier co-ordination and materials handling, seem to have been more complex than the assembly activities. Some of the component suppliers (the first category illustrated in Figure 3.8) not only supplied components for the T2–trucks but also various components for the other truck models produced by SweFork. Hence, several activity chains were channelled through the same supplier relationship, which made the situation complicated since SweFork felt a need to control these purchases and relationships.

Concerning the specific components, tools were used in the production of some of them, making it very difficult to change supplier. Either new tools had to be developed with considerable investments needed as a consequence, or the tools had to be moved. When the tools were moved from one supplier to another, this often required their being changed to fit into the machines used. Hence it would have been difficult for Industrial

Plastics not to hold on to these suppliers if they were made responsible for the purchasing of these components.

Other components were not (yet) produced using any specific tools. Some of these could, however, be manufactured at a lower cost per item if tools were developed and if the volumes were large enough, which could not be known in advance. If Industrial Plastics were to become responsible for these purchases, these cost considerations would become their concern. Because of the volume interdependence involved in these decisions, one relevant question was: who should take the risks and who should have the profits? Apart from the risks associated with the volumes, Industrial Plastics would also face the risk that SweFork would change the design of these components. Moreover, increasing the number of components produced using specific tools would affect the cost structure in terms of set-up costs (for the component suppliers) and lower costs per item, resulting in stock increases for Industrial Plastics. There were already a few components delivered just once per year.

In addition to these problems, the quality problems experienced by some component suppliers in combination with Industrial Plastics' efforts to become a certified ISO 9000 supplier complicated the situation further.

All this meant that SweFork would probably maintain its control over the purchasing of the components, with the possible exception of a few less important standard components only used in this particular steering arm. If so, Industrial Plastics would only be used as a resource unit activated by the injection moulding and the assembly activities needed to create the handles, and SweFork would control all supplier relationships and purchases involved (see Figure 3.9). As a result, the gains achieved by out-sourcing the handles would be low, since the way the activities were organised would require an increased need for co-ordination among the suppliers compared with undertaking the system assembly in-house. Extensive co-ordination would be required in order to handle the various kinds of interdependence related to time, volumes, technical connections and costs among the activities carried out by all the parties involved. In addition, the low degree of similarity that could be benefited from in Industrial Plastics' refining activities, mentioned above, did not contribute to the efficiency of this solution, at least not at the time. The way in which the activities would be organised is shown in Figure 3.9.

The reasons for the situation illustrated in Figure 3.9 are mainly related to the process, and to SweFork's need for control. Activity links that were difficult to break had been established by SweFork and the component suppliers during the process to solve certain problems. These links would have been difficult for Industrial Plastics to take on, and even if these problems could have been solved there would probably have been difficulties in using these suppliers in activity chains directed towards other

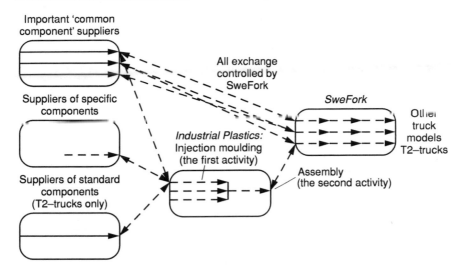

Figure 3.9 Organisation of activities after out-sourcing

customers. Therefore, Industrial Plastics could not, and in some instances SweFork would not allow them to, develop its own activity links to suppliers. SweFork's need for control was partly a desire to maintain its own activity links (and good supplier relationships in general) since these were also used in the production of other truck models.

What if Industrial Plastics or any other system supplier had been made fully responsible for development and the production of the handle, or the whole steering arm, from the outset? For one thing, this would have enabled establishment of, or use of existing, activity links to component suppliers. This would also have increased the system supplier's possibilities to utilise these links in activity chains directed towards other customers. If the system supplier was, as Industrial Plastics was, producing one or several of the critical components in the system, this firm could also be assumed to be better suited to handle the connections among its own components and others.

Summary

This case illustrates several aspects of the difficulties in reorganising activity structures. Various kinds of interdependence were created in the development of the steering arm, mainly resulting from efforts to solve the numerous technical problems that appeared during the process. This technical interdependence not only created restraints by its very existence; the knowledge of its presence and nature was also critical, and resulted in a perceived need for control from SweFork. By maintaining control over the relationships activated, the need for co-ordination of activities could not be reduced as a result of the out-sourcing but increased instead as one additional actor became involved in the activity structure. Furthermore, the activity subject to out-sourcing, i.e., assembly, was dissimilar from the other activities undertaken both by SweFork and Industrial Plastics. However, Industrial Plastics seemed to have better potential for achieving similarities in a long term perspective. Whether these potential gains will exceed the costs incurred by the extensive co-ordination remains to be seen.

The complete fork carriage

The complete fork carriage consisted of about thirty components of different sizes and values, bought from about twenty different suppliers. Eight of the components accounted for more than 80 per cent of the total component purchase value included in the system, and one component alone accounted for about 40 per cent of the total value. This component – the fork – was the main component in the system. Forks were used in all the truck models produced by SweFork but because of their various sizes, different production techniques and, therefore, different suppliers were used in production.

The complete fork carriage developed for the T2–truck mainly consisted of components made of heavy steel plates which were cut, bent, welded, assembled and painted. In addition, some standardised components of small value were either welded or assembled into it. The value of the entire system was high compared with the other systems. The size of the components made the pre-assembly of the complete fork carriages bulky, heavy and difficult to handle without special equipment. Therefore, some jigs were developed by SweFork to facilitate assembly.

When the T2–truck was developed, about six suppliers were asked for quotations on the forks. Some of them already supplied SweFork with other components, while others were new. One previously unknown supplier was involved and tested at an early stage. However, these tests showed unsatisfactory results in terms of technical function – the forks were not stable enough. Furthermore, this supplier, situated in the north of Sweden, was considered too far away once it was decided that the forks should be bought on end customer orders, necessitating a short geographical distance between the firms. A supplier who had been producing the forks for another small truck model, and thus already used a similar production technique, was not particularly interested in taking on the forks for the T2–trucks, owing to new priorities and a consequent lack of capacity. A supplier from Hungary was also considered. This supplier was much cheaper than the Swedish suppliers but its performance in terms of deliveries and quality was considered uncertain. Furthermore, using this supplier would have made it difficult and probably inefficient to out-source the complete fork carriages since this supplier could not be used as a system supplier for several reasons. Ultimately, a subcontractor of some of the other Swedish vehicle producers was found. SweFork considered these customer relationships a guarantee of quality and delivery reliability.

The potential system supplier – HMW

The system supplier, henceforth referred to as Heavy Machining Workshop (HMW), was founded in the 1920s as a producer of horse-shoes. When this market decreased, production successively changed to other products. Snowploughs and street-sweeping machines had long been its main products. As early as the 1940s HMW became a subcontractor of one of the large Swedish vehicle manufacturers. This part of the business had grown since then and the relationship with the vehicle manufacturer had developed. In the early 1990s, when the relationship with SweFork was established, HMW's subcontracting business accounted for about 50 per cent of its turnover of about SEK 65 million, and the large vehicle manufacturer had become its dominant source of income. At that time HMW had six customers on a subcontracting basis. The dominant customer alone accounted for 75 per cent of the subcontracting part of HMW's business. In order to reduce its dependency on this customer HMW strove to expand the exchange with the other five customers, who were roughly equally important in terms of purchase value – approximately SEK 1–2 million each.

The six subcontracting customers were quite large firms in comparison with HMW. Four of them were vehicle manufacturers, two of which were producers of heavy trucks; the other two, of which SweFork was one, produced lighter trucks for short distance materials handling. The other two customers also produced heavy equipment. The length of the customer relationships ranged from four to fifty years. The number of components produced for the individual customers varied between five and one hundred. Furthermore, all the customers sent delivery plans to HMW and order-based production constantly increased in favour of forecast planned production. Delivery frequency was about once or twice per week to each customer, and the time from definite order to delivery varied between four days and two weeks. HMW kept safety stocks for all their customers since the customers' production was very sensitive to disturbances. If HMW defaulted on its deliveries, the customers' production processes would be severely affected.

The subcontracting customers were considered very demanding. Continuous cost reductions were required by them, e.g., one required that the costs should be reduced by 15 per cent over a two year period. For this reason HMW was constantly trying to find new materials, production techniques, methods and designs to be able to achieve the cost reduction goals set by its customers. For instance, HMW suggested to one of its customers that pressing should be used instead of gas cutting and welding. In another case, it suggested that standardised profiles should be used instead of cut and bent steel plate. By effecting these changes, the costs could be reduced for both parties. One general problem experienced by HMW was that it was involved too late in the customers' development processes. This often resulted in the customers, in co-operation with HMW, having to redesign parts of their products to enable HMW to utilise its most efficient production techniques. These redesigning processes were considered costly and complex to handle for all involved parties.

Most of the material purchased by HMW was standardised raw material such as heavy steel plate, pipes and bars. Owing to the large volumes bought, HMW had been able to develop direct relationships with a few steel works, although some material was purchased from distributors nearby because of shorter lead times. Most of the raw material could be used for all of HMW's customers and also in its own products.

HMW's activities

The activities undertaken by HMW consisted mainly of various machining activities such as blending, cutting, bending, pressing, milling, drilling, turning, threading and welding. Some of these activities activated general work stations. In other words, the same equipment could be used in the production of all products requiring that activity, for instance blending. In a few cases, entirely customer specific work stations had been developed, such as automatic welding stations with welding robots, fixtures, etc. For the rest of the activities, a combination of general resources, such as machines and personnel, and specific resources, such as tools, jigs and fixtures, were used.

The sequence of activities often began with blending the raw materials before any machining activity could begin, owing to the fact that the raw material bought was covered with oxide scale. The blending was undertaken in the same way, and using the same equipment, for all components produced. Blending was thus the first activity in all activity chains handled by HMW. Although a blended steel plate could be used in several activity chains, the blending activity was not initiated unless an order had been received from a customer. Hence, in this respect, the blending activity was the first specific activity in all the different activity chains (unless the raw material used was specific to a certain activity chain, in which case the purchasing activity was the start of that specific activity chain).

After the blending had been completed, some cutting activity was usually undertaken. The cutting technique depended on the thickness of the material. For the thicker dimensions, gas cutting was required, while ordinary cutting and shearing tools could be used for the other dimensions.

However, both these techniques could be regarded as general in terms of the resources used, as they could be used in activity chains directed towards all customers.

Thereafter, some components required pressing, which was done using component specific tools. The machines in which the tools were used were general, and as such could be used in all activity chains in which pressing was included.

Milling, drilling, turning and threading were mostly undertaken in NC-machines which were general, although component specific programs had to be developed and used in them. This also made them flexible in terms of adjustments compared, for instance, with component specific tools, jigs and fixtures, which were less flexible and, thus, more complex to adjust.

Welding could be the next production step in an activity chain directed towards a certain customer. HMW had several welding stations, some of which were general in terms of equipment and personnel, although component specific fixtures were used within them. A few of the welding stations were entirely customer specific, since there were production volumes large enough to occupy them full time. For this reason HMW had been able to develop them into fully automatised work stations using robots.

At that time, assembly operations were only undertaken on HMW's own products but a few of the subcontracting customers, including SweFork, were considered interesting as potential system customers, which would enable HMW to enhance the utilisation of the assembly station. Since the assembly of heavy machine parts was difficult to handle, various types of support equipment were developed to facilitate assembly. HMW had thus specialised both in terms of skills and equipment in assembly of heavy machine parts.

Painting was also done, but at the time of the study only of HMW's own products, for several reasons. Two of the subcontracting customers had very high demands on the painting, which was not perceived by HMW to be possible for them to satisfy. Components that had to be painted at this stage of production therefore had to be sent to painting specialists approved by the customers, after which they were returned to HMW for milling, etc. before delivery to the customers.

HMW hoped that if they became responsible for the production of whole systems this would enhance its possibilities to be made responsible for the development of these systems as well. Through this, adjustments of both the systems and the components included could be made to suit its production methods better.

The relationship between HMW and SweFork

HMW produced several of the heaviest components, in terms of weight and value, in the complete fork carriage, and seemed to have assembly capabilities. Therefore, HMW was 'the natural' choice when it came to out-sourcing the whole system, and a test order for ten complete fork carriages was agreed upon. The evaluation of HMW's performance in this test order led to the following conclusions.

First, HMW proved to be able to assemble the complete fork carriage in half the time it took SweFork. This was explained by the fact that HMW's assembly work station was better adjusted to this kind of assembly than SweFork, with its more general assembly stations. For instance, the support equipment developed facilitated the work considerably. Moreover, by developing the assembly jigs, borrowed from SweFork, HMW expected that it would be able to reduce the assembly time even more.

Secondly, after studying the other components involved, HMW suggested that several of them could be made by HMW at lower costs than the current suppliers charged. A few of the other components, mainly standard components of minor value, were also bought by HMW for other purposes and could be purchased in larger volumes by them than SweFork. Moreover, HMW suggested that SweFork could use HMW's contracts for these components whenever they were favourable.

Thirdly, to facilitate internal transportation of the forks at the HMW workshop, carriers were developed. These also proved to be useful in carrying the whole system, and the use of the carriers could be extended to facilitate external transportation and internal materials handling at the SweFork workshop.

Fourthly, HMW could paint the complete fork carriages. HMW's painting facilities used drying ovens, which made the drying process faster. Moreover, although paint was bought from the same supplier as SweFork, lower paint prices had been obtained by HMW. At this time, ordinary paint was usually used both by SweFork and its suppliers, but an increasingly important goal for SweFork was to replace the ordinary paint with two-component paint, which was both more expensive and more complicated to apply. HMW proved to be willing and able to develop its painting to use two-component paint. SweFork appreciated this, since the painted complete fork carriages could then be sent directly into the final assembly of the T2–trucks at SweFork's workshop.

Analysis of the activity structure

All in all, about 150 customer specific subcontracted components were manufactured by HMW. Since all components were made mainly from standardised raw material, this meant that 150 specific activity chains directed towards six customers began in HMW's production processes. In principle, the activity structure of which HMW was a part can be illustrated as in Figure 3.10.

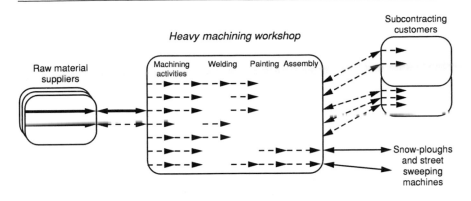

Figure 3.10 Activity structure in which HMW was involved

In addition to the subcontracted end products, HMW's own products also constituted specific activity chains. These resulted in standardised products, i.e., they were not subject to specific adaptations to the customers using them nor were they further refined.

The degree of similarity of the activity chains handled by HMW varied among the individual activities, and also in terms of what activities were included in the different chains. There was a high degree of similarity in terms of raw materials used, and therefore also in purchasing. In addition, the exchange activities, determined by the communication routines, delivery conditions, quality requirements and so on, directed towards the different customers seemed to be subject to a high degree of similarity.

The customers controlled the designs of the components produced for them by HMW. This restricted HMW's possibilities of connecting the chains, i.e., of taking advantage of similarities in the performance of individual activities. Therefore, HMW frequently encouraged the customers to redesign their components so that HMW would be able to use 'the right' production methods to carry out the activities efficiently. Redesigning the components might affect related components, which had to be dealt with by the customers and their other suppliers.

HMW produced several of the heaviest components included in the complete fork carriage. It seemed willing to take on other components included in the system in its own production. In addition, several standard components of minor value were already purchased by HMW in large volumes, resulting in volume purchasing benefits. Hence, various benefits could be taken advantage of by out-sourcing the whole system, apart from HMW's apparently higher efficiency in the assembling activity.

Figure 3.11 is a comparison of the activity structures in which SweFork assembled the complete fork carriages (Figure 3.11.a) compared with if they had been out-sourced to HMW (Figure 3.11.b).

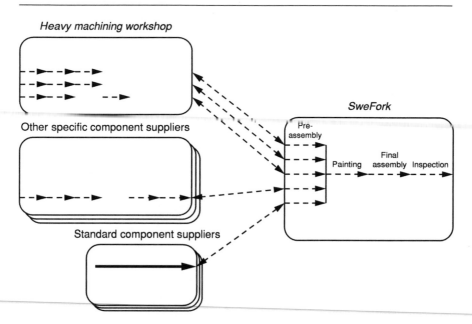

Figure 3.11.a Activity structure related to complete fork carriage before outsourcing

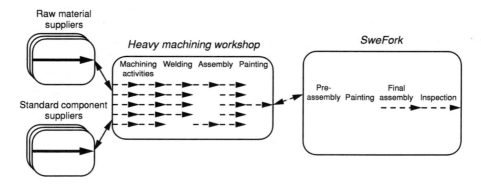

Figure 3.11.b Activity structure related to complete fork carriage after outsourcing

In letting HMW take on the whole system, SweFork would only have to handle one supplier instead of about twenty, which would reduce both their purchasing and materials handling activities. Since there were similarities among the activity chains handled by HMW in terms of these activities, the total exchange activities in the activity structure resulting in the complete fork carriage could be reduced.

The sequence of activities undertaken was not changed in this case and therefore the intended change was mainly to move some transformation activities, i.e., assembly and painting, to HMW. These transformation activities could be connected to other activity chains at HMW. Assembly could be done in half the time by HMW as by SweFork, thanks to the similarity between this assembly activity and HMW's assembly of its own products. The degree of similarity among the systems pre assembled by SweFork was low. Furthermore, painting could be done by HMW using the same equipment as used in production of its own products. The use of these resources could be extended to other customers in the future, which would enhance efficiency even further.

Summary

This case illustrates how efficiency potentials could be taken advantage of by moving certain activities from SweFork to one of its suppliers. These efficiency potentials stemmed from the similarities among the activities subject to movement and those already undertaken by the supplier. Furthermore, the supplier seemed to be able to (a) adapt certain specific resources to increase the efficiency in the performance, and (b) in a longer perspective adapt its general resources even further to increase resource sharing among the activity chains organised within its boundaries.

In a long-term perspective, additional gains could be achieved by letting the supplier take on the responsibility for design, including choice of materials and production techniques. This would further enhance the supplier's possibilities to develop and take advantage of similarities among activities directed towards its different customers.

The machine body

One important section of the truck is the machine body. A machine body consists of sixteen parts, some of which can be classified as raw material, others as standard components and still others as custom designed components. Different truck models have different types of machine bodies, and different suppliers produce the components. Basically, the same activities are needed for all truck models from the purchasing of the machine body parts to the final assembly, during which the machine body is assembled with other systems to make a complete truck. The other activities consist of several machining operations (such as cutting, drilling and bending) of some of the parts, a welding operation (in which the parts are put together) and a painting operation.

For one of the truck models, the machine bodies were made in-house by SweFork until the late 1980s (phase 1), when they were out-sourced to a supplier who supplied the company with complete machine bodies (phase

2). About five years later, the make-or-buy decision was reconsidered and the machine bodies were in-sourced (phase 3). The impact of these choices on the organisation of the activities is described below.

Phase 1: Component purchasing and in-house production

During phase 1 the chain of activities carried out by SweFork was divided into five steps.

1 Six pre-machined steel plates and ten additional components were bought from different suppliers.
2 The steel plates were manually welded to the additional components.
3 The machine bodies were painted with primer.
4 The machine bodies were assembled with other systems.
5 Top coat painting, including masking of certain areas, was undertaken.

Paint always has to be applied before assembly to cover all parts of the steel plates in order to prevent corrosion. Two coats of paint, primer and top coat, were necessary, as ordinary paint was used at the time. Owing to the low quality of the paint, a top coat had to be added after assembly since the painted surfaces would otherwise have been damaged. The process was costly because the top coat painting job required masking. The results suffered in terms of quality since paint got stuck in the cavities, causing defects. The in-house welding operations, which were manual at the time, were also a constant source of trouble. Concerning purchasing and materials handling, the sixteen parts in the system were bought from about ten suppliers and were stocked in the central supply store. The supplier of the pre-machined steel plates used conventional machining

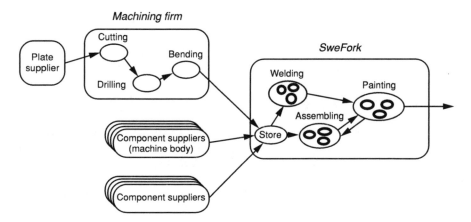

Figure 3.12 Organisation of activities during phase 1

equipment. Figure 3.12 shows the transformation activities undertaken by the companies involved and the flows between their respective work stations.

Phase 2: System sourcing

In the late 1980s, the machine body was out-sourced to a system supplier – Systech – who had invested heavily in the installation of a flexible manufacturing system (FMS) and was, at the time, eager to fill this capacity. In addition, Systech could offer two-component painting which, thanks to its high quality, only required one coat of paint, put on before assembly. In order not to damage the painted surfaces, and also to facilitate assembly, SweFork developed assembly jigs. One of the prerequisites for the two-component paint is a drying oven, since it would otherwise take days for the paint to dry. As it turned out, however, Systech had an external painting firm do the work on SweFork's machine bodies because of capacity shortage at its own factory. The welding operations were done in exactly the same way by Systech as had previously been done by SweFork. The welding fixtures used by SweFork were thus transferred to Systech. Figure 3.13 shows how the activities were organised during phase 2.

Systech purchased fourteen of the components of the machine body. The remaining two were bought from SweFork's suppliers on SweFork's contracts, since SweFork also bought large volumes of these components for use in other truck models. For the fourteen components bought by Systech, similar parts within the systems produced for other customers could be used, resulting in economies of scale in purchasing.

When painted items are transported, problems arise since the items are easily damaged. When the machine bodies were out-sourced, this problem was solved by using a special container offered at the time by a transportation firm. These small containers were a perfect fit, and made it

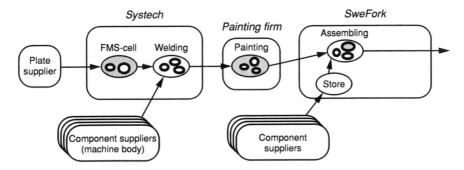

Figure 3.13 Organisation of activities during phase 2

possible to transport 'the right' quantities at low costs without wrapping. Packaging is otherwise very costly since the machine bodies are bulky and difficult to package. A few years later, the transport firm withdrew these containers, owing to general lack of demand. This made transportation, which now had to be undertaken on ordinary lorries, more costly because of additional wrapping material and packaging.

Phase 3: In-sourcing

About five years after the decision to buy machine bodies from Systech, SweFork decided to in-source some of the activities. In the early 1990s SweFork had invested in two-component painting equipment including ovens, which made it possible to carry out painting in-house. The machining activities could not be undertaken by SweFork, and since Systech handled them well, these activities were still to be purchased from Systech. It was also considered efficient to get whole sets of machine body parts from Systech. These sets could then go directly into SweFork's welding station without having to be handled by the central supply store, keeping internal logistics at a low level. When the in-sourcing decision was discussed, the question of manual welding versus robot welding arose. Since there was excess robot station capacity, and since robots would achieve faster welding, this alternative was chosen. However, some manual welding would still be required because welding spots had to be added in the welding fixture before robots could take over. Figure 3.14 shows this reorganisation of the activities.

At about the same time as SweFork in-sourced the welding and painting activities, the demand for this particular truck model fluctuated, and even decreased dramatically. Earlier on, the production volumes were high and fairly constant. SweFork's delivery plans were based on sales forecasts and up-dated every third month. The forecasts had previously matched actual orders (which were based on end customer orders) sent three weeks prior to delivery. When the demand for the trucks began to decrease, the gap between the delivery plans and the actual orders widened. This led to problems for Systech, where both purchasing and production activities had been adapted to the previous volumes and delivery frequency. For one thing, the steel plates, bought in special formats from a German steel works, had to be ordered twelve weeks prior to delivery. The materials planner at Systech had continued to make the call-offs in accordance with the forecasts, i.e., based on SweFork's delivery plans, which resulted in an increasing stock of plates. Other parts in the machine bodies, although of less value and subject to shorter lead times than the steel plates, were subcontracted by Systech. The subcontractors also based their purchasing and production activities on SweFork's delivery plans. This led to a situation in which SweFork's machine body specific materials and components

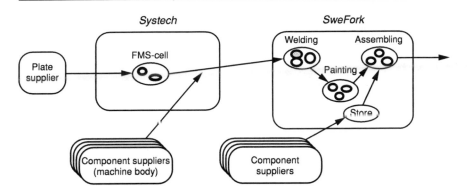

Figure 3.14 Organisation of activities during phase 3

were kept in stock for long periods in several layers of suppliers. When this situation was exposed, Systech demanded that the ordering routines be revised.

The current production volumes were not considered to warrant special format steel plates to be purchased directly from the German steel works. Instead, standard format plates stocked and delivered by a steel distributor could be used. Systech bought standard plates from this distributor on a regular basis with deliveries twice a week. Systech could thus possibly keep the standard format plates in stock to further increase availability. This decision, however, required that the same steel plates (in terms of material and thickness) could be used by other customers. The standard plates also needed to be cut into the required format. This could be done either by the distributor or by Systech.

The time from order to delivery needed to be lengthened from the current three weeks to six weeks so that all production and purchasing activities undertaken by Systech could be based on actual orders from SweFork. Since SweFork's delivery time to their customers was four weeks, this would result in a situation in which SweFork would have to handle a certain stock of machine body parts, and it would be impossible to send these parts straight to the welding unit as planned.

The companies involved

Companies other than SweFork and Systech also influenced the flow of events in the relationship of the two companies. The activities undertaken by these other companies affected the efficiency of the arrangements of the two firms vis-à-vis one another. Figure 3.15 shows the other actors influencing the efficiency in the relationship between SweFork and Systech.

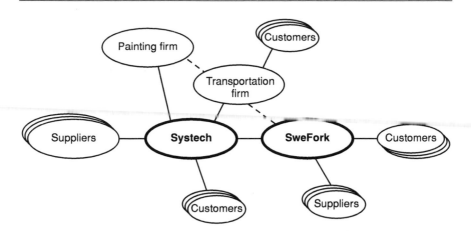

Figure 3.15 The companies involved and the relationships among them

SweFork's perspective

No efforts had been made to co-ordinate the sourcing of the different machine bodies, although basically the same activities were needed (the main differences between the machine bodies were differences of size dimensions). Sourcing solutions were chosen each time a major change was made in a truck model or when a new model was developed. These major changes were made one at a time. The situation on each such occasion in terms, for instance, of capacity at SweFork's work stations determined what was to be done in-house and what was to be out-sourced. When making the cost calculations, only the cost per unit was taken into account; neither the costs incurred from making the changes nor the cost effects on other activities were considered. Furthermore, in times of excess capacity, the labour cost per hour was set at half the actual cost, which spoke in favour of in-sourcing decisions.

All the work stations activated to produce SweFork's machine bodies were shared with activities performed on other parts of the trucks. One of these parts was considered the core part of the truck, and was therefore always produced in-house and ranked highest in priority. Therefore, in times of capacity shortage, other parts or systems were out-sourced.

In SweFork's view, the supplier market had been developing over the years. Numerous suppliers were able to undertake the crucial activities. However, during recent years the suppliers had been divided into two categories: one consisting of small firms using conventional equipment (like the machining firm used in phase 1) and the other of comparably larger firms using modern equipment and production methods (like Systech). By focusing on large and demanding customers such as the

Swedish heavy truck manufacturers, the latter category had been forced to offer J-I-T (just-in-time) deliveries, guaranteeing high quality (ISO 9000 was required by the customers), etc. The former category's resources were affected by their cost structure (low fixed costs) enabling these firms to be more flexible in reacting to variations in volumes. Therefore, a few of these firms had been able to offer lower prices for some of the machine bodies than the larger firms. Since the smaller firms were seldom able to offer two-component painting, this activity had to be undertaken either by SweFork or by an external painting firm. In one such case extensive delivery problems occurred, and were further complicated by the fact that the supplier and the painting firm blamed one another for the inadequacies. In terms of the painting, one of the complications was getting the right shade on different surfaces. Therefore, one solution considered by SweFork was to concentrate all the painting that could not be done in-house to one or a few external painting firms, preferably close to the SweFork site. These firms could then also take on paint jobs for system suppliers with in-house painting problems. This solution would reduce the costs associated with solving the painting problems for several parties involved, and would also make it possible to better co-ordinate transportation.

The activities carried out by SweFork were subject to limitations in terms of capacity and also in the perceived need to control certain activities in-house. Concerning the machine bodies, the function of the suppliers was generally to handle variations in the production volume since SweFork's own capacity was rather fixed in activities such as welding and painting.

Systech's perspective

Systech was established in the 1950s and was acquired and restructured by the present owners in the mid-1980s. The most important customers were among the largest manufacturing firms in Sweden, e.g., several companies within the Volvo group, Ericsson and ABB. Most of the customer relationships had been established in the late 1980s. Since then they had been developing mainly in terms of communication routines and of co-ordinated technical development. Information technology solutions were applied to facilitate production planning both internally (an MPS-system was used) and externally (the customers were increasingly sending their delivery plans by EDI). Thus, the flow of information from the customers was, in a few cases, integrated all the way from the customers' planning functions to the FMS-cell at Systech. CAD had been used internally for some time, and some of the customers had started sending their CAD-drawings electronically. Hence, one main concern had become integration of the information systems. This would entail less administration, reduced lead times and result in fewer errors in the process. However, the prerequisites for making this integration throughout depended on the ability of the customers to adjust to the new procedures. To achieve a fully integrated information flow, delivery plans from the customers would have to be received as EDI-files that could be updated more often than paper-based plans. Paper-based delivery plans were only updated, as in SweFork's case, once every three months.

For the customers to be able to benefit from these working procedures they had to use the same means of communication with their other suppliers. This was already the case with several of the main customers. Systech was increasingly involved in these customers' new product development processes. In some instances Systech had even been made fully responsible for the development of parts of the customers' products. This had contributed to reducing the customers' lead times concerning both development and production. The latter could be achieved by adapting the designs to fit the current production methods used by Systech.

Systech was investing in increased internal efficiency. Integrating the information flows, as has been described above, was one important way of rationalising the administrative work. Production techniques were also constantly subject to development. For example, spot welding had been replaced by butt (upset) riveting. Spot welding requires destructive tests, while riveting requires only that the butts be checked. An additional efficiency improvement was the way in which Systech constantly reconsidered what activities could be most efficiently taken care of in-house and what activities should be contracted to suppliers. Simple machining operations were subcontracted to smaller machining firms with less sophisticated production equipment. Hence, for capacity and cost reasons, Systech had built its own network of sub-suppliers. Other activities could not be performed efficiently in-house for reasons of volume or scale. One such activity subject to reconsideration was painting. The painting facilities on site consisted of two painting lines, one of which was adapted to suit some customers whose products were made in large volumes before the company was taken over by the present owners. However, the demand for these products had diminished, which had reduced the capacity utilisation on this painting line from full utilisation down to one and a half days per week. The second painting line, used to paint several customers' products, needed investments in a filter system, among other things, to comply with the current environmental regulations. To be used efficiently modern painting facilities need to be run on a three-shift basis. The current volumes did not permit this, especially since some of Systech's most important customers had specific requirements which forced all their suppliers to send their products to be painted by certified painting specialists. For this reason, Systech had already developed relationships with a few painting specialists capable of meeting the requirements and able to perform the painting at lower costs. All these reasons favoured a decision to out-source all painting activities to painting or surface-treatment specialists.

Analysis of the activity structure

One obvious reason for SweFork to initiate reorganisation of the activities during the three phases was the successive improvements of the resources used to perform the activities. The resource improvements affected the activities. First, they affected the costs of the individual activities to which the resources were connected. Secondly, the chain of activities reflected by the flow between work stations was affected. However, these rather straightforward effects of the improvements of the resources do not alone explain the changes in the division of labour in this case. In order to understand the 'whole picture' we have to include the other 'users' of the resources since they influenced the efficiency of the activities carried out. Therefore, the third issue that will be dealt with in the analysis of what happened during the three phases is how the specific machine body activities were related to other activities sharing the same resources. The changes in volume and delivery frequency occurring in phase 3 revealed aspects of the activity structure which had not been obvious previously. The fourth aspect that will be dealt with in the analysis concerns the question of how the reduction in the volumes affected the activity chain and the individual activities of several actors. Fifthly, the previous time interdependence in the activity structure could not be handled in a situation characterised by uncertainty and fluctuating demand. This also called for changes in the activity structure involving several actors. Lastly, some development issues affecting the efficiency of the activity structure in which Systech and its counterparts were involved will be discussed.

Changes of individual activities

The resource improvements made during the three phases are summarised in Table 3.2.

    If we look at the situation in phase 1, in which the machine bodies were manufactured in-house, and compare it with phase 3, we can see that all the individual activities have gone through changes. First, purchasing could be done on a larger scale by Systech (from phase 1 to 2). Secondly, the machining operations could be made more efficient using Systech's FMS-cell (from phase 1 to 2). The advantages achieved within these two activities could be maintained in phase 3, since Systech was still going to be responsible for these activities. Thirdly, welding could be made more efficient, owing to the shift from manual to robot welding (from phase 2

Table 3.2   Activities performed and resources used by SweFork and Systech

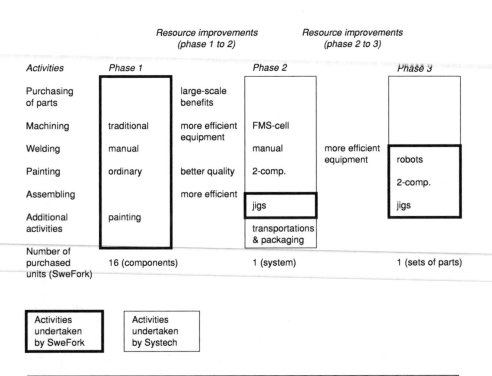

Activities	Phase 1	Resource improvements (phase 1 to 2)	Phase 2	Resource improvements (phase 2 to 3)	Phase 3
Purchasing of parts		large-scale benefits			
Machining	traditional	more efficient equipment	FMS-cell		
Welding	manual		manual	more efficient equipment	robots
Painting	ordinary	better quality	2-comp.		2-comp.
Assembling		more efficient			
Additional activities	painting		jigs		jigs
			transportations & packaging		
Number of purchased units (SweFork)	16 (components)		1 (system)		1 (sets of parts)

Activities undertaken by SweFork	Activities undertaken by Systech

to 3). Fourthly, the painting activity became more efficient when a switch was made from ordinary to two-component painting (from phase 1 to 2), which was maintained in phase 3 thanks to the investments made by SweFork. Fifthly, assembly could be made more efficient owing to the jigs that were developed (from phase 1 to 2). Furthermore, additional activities could be eliminated successively: the extra painting activity (from phase 1 to 2), and the extra transportation and packaging activities (from phase 2 to 3). For SweFork, internal logistics were considerably reduced when the machine bodies were out-sourced, since only one item had to be handled. This low degree of materials handling could be maintained almost entirely in phase 3 since Systech was supplying sets of parts.

Changes in the chain of activities and the flow between the work stations

The activities were all sequentially interdependent, i.e., machining could not be done after welding, and painting could not be done before welding, etc. The main advantages of out-sourcing the machine bodies in phase 2 were related to Systech's resources: the FMS-cell used for machining, and the two-component painting facilities. Therefore the welding, which came in between the machining and the painting activities, was also out-sourced to Systech even though the welding operation was done in exactly the same way as before. One major change in terms of sequential dependencies among the activities in this case was that by raising the quality of the paint, the chain of activities could be changed – i.e., the extra painting activity (including masking) could be eliminated. Thus, the chain of activities was altered as some activities were changed, others were moved and still others were eliminated.

Changes regarding connections between activity chains and sharing of resources

All the resources (related to the work stations) used in this case were also used for other purposes than the machine bodies. For example, when the welding activity was performed by Systech, the welding unit was shared with activities performed for Systech's other customers. When the welding was done by SweFork the same resources were shared with the welding of other parts to be mounted into the same and other truck models.

SweFork could benefit from the advantages of scale Systech had been able to achieve by purchasing steel plates as well as other components, and thus also benefit from the relationships Systech had developed with their suppliers, including the painting firm. This, in turn, was naturally dependent on Systech's other customers who, because of the similarities in their needs, contributed to various extents to these advantages of scale. The degree to which each work station's capacity could be utilised influenced production costs. However, in times of capacity shortages, the activities directed towards different customers could compete to some extent, which would force Systech to choose among its customers. It seems natural that certain priorities would reflect the importance of the customers.

Some of Systech's other customers were considered very demanding. Among other things, they tried to pressure the suppliers into granting constant production cost reductions, many of which would also affect other customers. However, in order for these other customers to take advantage of the cost reduction potentials, adaptations would be required. These adaptations could be, for example, design changes and reconsiderations of raw material choices. Another obvious linking effect in terms of efficiency in phase 2 was the container solution, which had to be changed owing to lack of demand. This resulted in higher transport costs for SweFork, and reduced the benefits of buying the machine bodies from Systech.

SweFork did not seem to take full advantage of the similarity between the activities for the different machine bodies either internally by co-ordination of the activities, or externally, for instance by concentrating the activities to one system supplier. Both alternatives could contribute to an increase in the advantages of scale and give SweFork a better position vis-à-vis the system supplier. What was not considered in the cost estimates was the costs involved in making the changes. These costs were related to finding feasible suppliers, and establishing relationships with them in order to make the links between the firms' activities work smoothly. The costs were also related to different adjustments in the internal production activities and, in many instances, to making design changes in order to adapt to the suppliers' production equipment. This would have an impact on other parts of the truck, directly and indirectly related to the machine bodies.

Volume interdependence

To cope with the reduced production volume, the activity chain and the individual activities had to be reorganised. The steel plates had to be altered from special format plates to standard plates. In order to benefit from the use of the standard plates, a distributor was used. This also resulted in shorter lead times vis-à-vis the system supplier. Consequently, a purchasing activity had to be added to the activity chain since one additional relationship – to the distributor – came in between the steel works and Systech. The use of standard plates required the cutting activity to be moved from the steel works, either to the distributor or to Systech. On the whole, individual activities were either being changed, added, moved or eliminated as a result of the reorganisation. Consequently, the activities undertaken by the firms involved changed, as illustrated in Table 3.3.

The change affected the activity structure because it altered the extent to which the activity chain was specific to SweFork's machine body. Prior to the change, the chain of activities had been specific to SweFork, beginning

Table 3.3 Firms and activities influenced by the change

Firm	Activities	
	Before (high volume)	After (low volume)
Steel works	Production of special format steel plates	Production of standard steel plates
Distributor		Purchasing, storing, etc. Cutting (1)
Systech	Purchasing	Purchasing Cutting (2)

with the production of the steel plates at the steel works. After the change, the activity chain would be specific to SweFork either:

1   at the distributor – if the cutting activity was to be undertaken by the distributor, or
2a at Systech if the standard plates bought by Systech were used only to produce SweForks machine bodies, or
2b if the standard plates could be used for the production directed towards other customers which would mean that the cutting activity undertaken by Systech would delimit the start of the specific part of the activity chain.

In Figure 3.16, the activity chains before and after (the above three alternatives are considered) the reorganisation, and the actors involved, are presented.

The work stations activated by the specific activities were also used for other purposes, but the activities themselves were specific to SweFork and the production of its machine bodies.

One important aspect of scale was the other purposes to which the last general (non-specific) activity in the activity chain could be connected. In 1 and 2a this last general activity was the purchasing activity (including materials handling, etc.) undertaken by the distributor. One main consideration was the extent to which the standard steel plates could be used for other customers than Systech. If no other customers of the distributor needed the same standard plates there could still be advantages (in materials handling but not storage) associated with using the distributor if Systech used the distributor as a source of other purchases and/or if the distributor used the steel works as a source of other purchases. Another concern was who was best suited to cut the plates, the distributor or Systech? Once again this is a matter of whether and how the activity and the work station activated by the activity could be used for other purposes. In 2b the last general activity, purchasing, was done by Systech. This leads to the question of for what other purposes these particular steel plates could be used by Systech.

The activity chains depicted in Figure 3.16 may prove useful in the search for the advantages associated with making adjustments in the activity chain. Before the reorganisation of the activity chain, the specific part of the chain began in the production of the plates at the steel works. Hence, the choice of steel plates in terms of, for example, material composition and thickness could be made on certain premises related to (a) the capabilities of the steel producer, (b) the production methods used by Systech, and (c) the connections between the steel plates' characteristics and other parts of the truck. After the reallocation, certain adjustments in the choice of plates could increase the advantages of having the specific part of the activity chain shortened. By adjusting the choice of steel plates

Activities undertaken before the change

Activities undertaken after the change (alternative 1)

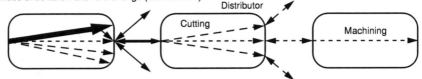

Activities undertaken after the change (alternative 2a)

Activities undertaken after the change (alternative 2b)

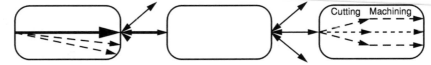

‑ ‑ ‑ ‑ ‑ ‑ ‑ ‑ ➤ Activities specific to SweFork's machine bodies

‑ ‑ ‑ ‑ ‑ ➤ Activities specific to other customers

The thickness of the arrows illustrates the differences in scale among the activities

Figure 3.16 Activity chains before and after their reorganisation

in accordance with as many other of Systech's customers as possible, benefits would be gained immediately and/or in a longer perspective. These benefits could be related to

1 the production methods used by Systech (related, in turn, to the flexibility of the work stations activated and the costs related to adjustments within the flexibility), and
2 availability, which could be related to the time dependencies in the activity structure.

Although there were indirect connections to the other customers prior to the reallocation, owing to shared resources, these connections and thus

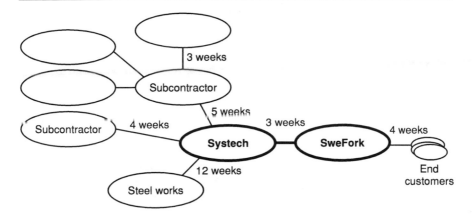

Figure 3.17 Time from order to delivery between some of the actors

the degree of similarity could become more direct. Here the connections between the characteristics of the steel plates and the other parts of the truck can be seen as restrictions on the adjustments.

Time interdependence

In connection with the volume reductions, the delivery frequency decreased and became irregular. This focused attention on the time interdependence among the activities (and thus between the companies performing them) in the activity chain. In Figure 3.17, the time interdependence (reflected by the time from order to delivery) among some of the actors involved in the specific part of the activity structure is illustrated.

The time interdependence in the activity structure required almost constant production volumes (or accurate forecasts) to make it manageable. The changes considered in order to cope with the problems caused by the time interdependence were of two kinds. By reducing the extent of the specific part of the activity chain, the time interdependence between some of the activities was eliminated, while in other cases it was reduced. For instance, by using standard plates and buying them from a distributor, the time associated with the purchasing of the steel plates could be cut down to one week or even be eliminated if the particular plates could be used on a scale permitting Systech to maintain its own stock. The other problem was that of adjusting the activity structure to being entirely based on actual orders from end customers. This meant that the time from order (SweFork's) to delivery (from Systech) would increase from three to six weeks. The consequences of extending this time were clearly negative from SweFork's perspective. A stock of machine bodies (or rather sets of parts for machine bodies) would be needed. This made it impossible to handle the flows as planned, i.e., having the machine body sets going directly into the welding unit. In order to avoid these inefficiencies, SweFork would have to increase its lead-times vis-à-vis its customers by two weeks.

Systech and its counterparts – development issues

The main focus at the time for Systech was three-fold;

1 To reduce the lead times in production.
2 To enhance the production planning in order to utilise as much of the production capacity as possible.
3 To become increasingly responsible for system solutions.

All three of these goals highlighted the need to co-operate closely with the customers. Systech considered the third point very important, and one of its main strengths. In order to be able to develop and produce systems efficiently, early involvement in the development process and preferably responsibilities for specified functions were considered necessary. This also required that Systech activated its own sub-suppliers and made 'the right' choices regarding who was best suited to perform the different activities needed. Moreover, it also often required that internal customer specific work stations, such as assembly and test stations, were developed. In one such case, Systech activated about twenty sub-suppliers for various machining and surface treatment activities and produced about thirty components in its own resource units. The components produced in-house required an average of eight operations per item. The components were welded and mounted together, and the resulting systems were, finally, painted and tested.

In order for Systech to increase its overall efficiency, an increasing degree of similarity of certain aspects related to the customers was required. One such aspect was the way in which the communication was handled, a second was technical development interaction, and a third important aspect was related to the extent to which the customers bought 'the right things'.

By increasing the use of information technology solutions in the communication with the customers, administrative resources could be eliminated in a longer term perspective. Interaction during new product development was necessary in order for Systech to increase the efficiency of individual activities. This enabled Systech to make continuous improvements of their production methods and to interconnect the activities performed towards the different customers within its resource units, so that high degrees of capacity utilisation could be achieved. In addition, the importance of *what* was bought from Systech was clear. In order for Systech to be able to utilise or activate as many of its resources as possible, system solutions were preferred since they let Systech activate combinations of internal and external resources. The internal resources consisted both of tangible resources, such as equipment and an experienced work force, and intangible resources, such as capabilities to create unique solutions for individual customers. The external resources that could be activated by Systech were found within the network of sub-suppliers of different kinds that had been developed. All these adjustments of the way of working between the customers and Systech could be beneficial for all parties involved if they were related to similar adjustments or consistent with adjustments in other relationships.

Hence, the relationships with the customers set the terms for Systech's development. Customers who did not fit into this development, or who did not contribute to the development by adjusting to it, disturbed the development path. The inefficiencies caused by a particular customer who did not fit into the ongoing development of Systech could, furthermore, grow as a result of other customers developing along with the supplier. For instance, if all but one customer were able to communicate their delivery plans and orders by EDI, the one customer persisting in sending paper-based plans and orders would force the supplier to maintain personnel and equipment to handle this customer manually. Thus, this customer would become 'expensive' if the resources needed to handle it could not be shared with others. In cost calculation terms, the costs for this administrative resource would have turned from having been shared among several customers and thus being included in the general overhead into a direct cost related to this customer.

All the customers who utilised Systech as a supplier had unique components or systems adjusted to their own activities, resources and to different technical dimensions of other parts of their end products. Efficient solutions could be created, since some resource units were shared and others were developed and used to suit individual customer needs. For example, some customers required that test stations be developed so that the component or system did not have to be inspected on arrival, but could go directly into production. Systech's willingness when it came to developing specific resources and activities to meet individual customers' requirements could be supposed to be dependent upon the extent to which a specific customer was considered to be able and willing to fit into the overall development, as described above. It can be assumed that a high degree of similarity in certain respects was a prerequisite for Systech's willingness to adapt its existing resources, or to develop new specific resources, for individual customers.

All this emphasises the interconnectedness among the activity links within the relationships shown in Figure 3.15. What could be done for one particular customer in terms of efficiency was highly dependent upon what was done for the other customers, which was dependent in turn upon how the customers' other supplier relationships were handled.

Chapter 4

Interdependence in activity structures

The case presented in the previous chapter illustrates the different ways in which activities are interrelated. First, vertical interdependence among the activities gives them an activity structure converging into the complete T2–truck (see Figure 4.1).

Secondly, there is horizontal interdependence among activities belonging to a certain end product related activity structure, such as the one illustrated in Figure 4.1, and other activity structures, owing to the fact that the activities activate common resources in different ways and to different extents. Therefore, alternative ways of organising activities with activities belonging to other activity structures, i.e., of creating and capturing similarities among them, are important with respect to efficiency.

Hence, when focusing on the organising of activity structures, vertical and horizontal interdependence are two features of activities that need to be included. However, these activity based interdependence aspects do not capture all the complexity since the resources that are activated and produced in an activity structure are not independent. Two resource based interdependence categories therefore also need to be included in the analysis of interdependence within activity structures: technical interdependence among resources, and interdependence created by the firms as 'pools' or 'bundles' of resources. These constitute the third and fourth interdependence aspects dealt with in this chapter.

Technical interdependence can be found between resources and products activated and produced within activity structures. Although it sometimes follows the vertical and horizontal interdependence among activities, technical interdependence also frequently cuts across activity structures, adding to the difficulties in organising them.

The firm as a 'pool' of resources has been touched upon previously as the third dimension of analysis in the analytical framework. Here we take a closer look at the consequences of firms for the interdependence of activity structures and thus for the organisation of activities within them.

In this chapter these four interdependence aspects are further elaborated based on illustrations found in, or inspired by, the SweFork case.

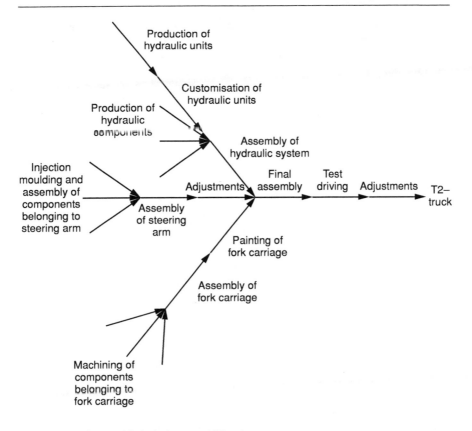

Production of
hydraulic units

Customisation of
hydraulic units

Production of
hydraulic
components

Assembly of
hydraulic system

Injection
moulding and
assembly of
components
belonging to
steering arm

Assembly
of steering
arm

Adjustments

Final
assembly

Test
driving

Adjustments

T2–
truck

Painting of
fork carriage

Assembly of
fork carriage

Machining of
components
belonging to
fork carriage

Note: The final assembly includes an additional
number of systems and components.

Figure 4.1 Fragment of activity structure resulting in complete T2–trucks

In particular, the two latter interdependence aspects are expanded on, as
they complicate the rather straightforward activity interdependence dealt
with in the framework.

VERTICAL INTERDEPENDENCE

Vertical interdependence reflects sequential interdependence among activities. Hence, each activity in an activity structure can be described in terms
of the activities undertaken before and after it. Thus, the individual
activities embedded in an end product related activity structure are all
directly or indirectly dependent on other activities in terms of sequence.
Furthermore, activity chains typically merge in an activity structure, and
therefore parallel interdependence among activities belonging to chains

which merge at a later stage can be identified. In addition, time inter-dependence among activities undertaken in sequence and in parallel can be identified. Hence, vertical interdependence is directly associated with sequential, parallel and time interdependence among activities within an end product related activity structure.

In Figure 4.1 a fragment of the activity structure resulting in the T2–truck is illustrated. The chains resulting in components for the hydraulic system, the steering arm and the complete fork carriage respectively are merged at certain points in the structure. Thereafter, one or two activities are under-taken in the three chains resulting in the systems which then are merged in the final assembly activity. Finally, test driving and adjustments are also carried out prior to the truck's completion.

However, the sequence is not technologically 'given'. Rather, there are often alternative ways of organising activities vertically. For instance, the SweFork case illustrates how the organisation of activities into the T2–truck was adapted to the system sourcing intentions. The production of older trucks based on integrated designs was characterised by more or less successive addition of components to the chains resulting in the trucks. In the production of the system design based T2–truck, each of the systems was instead first put together separately and then merged in a final assembly activity (see Figure 4.1).

Changing one activity may impact on other activities in the chain and/or the sequence in which the activities are undertaken. This can be illustrated by the machine body case in which the painting activity was subject to change. Owing to the better quality of the painting result from the two-component paint, the painting activity undertaken after assembly, which was needed when using primer and top-coat paints, could be eliminated.

Other aspects of a sequential nature illustrated by the SweFork case were the considerations concerning where in the chain the testing or inspection activities should be. Having these activities organised late in the chain meant that certain faults had to be corrected several steps up the chain and also that the faulty parts typically contained a large number of components. The alternative was to organise testing and inspection activities at an earlier stage in the chain to find the faults closer to the activity or activities causing them, which would also impact positively on the requisites for correcting or adjusting the activity if necessary.

Obviously, vertical interdependence has to be considered when activities are reorganised among firms. The machine body case may be used as an example. When SweFork decided to utilise the supplier's FMS-cell and two component painting facilities, the welding activity was also moved to the supplier since this activity was undertaken between the machining and the painting activities. That is, although there were no gains perceived in out-sourcing the welding activity *per se*, it was out-sourced owing to the fact that it was subject to vertical interdependence to two other activities undertaken before and after it. Hence, even if there had been disadvantages associated with the movement of this particular activity, for instance in terms of suffering capacity utilisation in SweFork's own welding equipment, there could have been overall advantages in outsourcing the activity as one of several in the activity chain of concern.

HORIZONTAL INTERDEPENDENCE

In order to perform an individual activity a set of resources – referred to as a resource unit – is activated. Each resource unit consists of physical and human resources bound together with reference to a certain activity. Some of the resource units are immobile as they are fixed in certain places. Furthermore, each resource unit is limited in terms of capacity and of the type of activities that can be performed. Therefore, two important characteristics are the capacity and flexibility of each resource unit.

Some resource units activated within an activity structure may be fully utilised by one activity within it, while others have to be shared to be efficiently utilised. If resource units are shared among several activities the cost for the performance of each individual activity is determined by the costs of the resources that are consumed in the process, and the activity's share of the activated resources. Hence, the cost associated with each individual activity is dependent on the total capacity utilisation of the resource unit and its scale properties. Capacity utilisation is, in turn, dependent upon the resource unit's flexibility. Resource development may consequently affect the potential efficiency of an activity structure since the capacity and the flexibility, and thus the prerequisites for capacity utilisation, may be altered. In the machine body case several examples can be found. The FMS-cell replaced manual machining equipment which meant that three activities (cutting, drilling and bending) were replaced by one activity, activating a resource unit with a higher degree of flexibility. On the other hand, the welding activity, which was altered from manual to robot operated, activated a less flexible resource unit as a result of the change. However, both these changes entailed increased efficiency, but the increased efficiency in both cases was dependent on the other activities activating the resource units. Therefore, the flexibility of a resource unit is always a relative measure among the activities activating it. And since capacity is decisive to the activities' total utilisation of it, the flexibility and capacity of a resource unit are highly interrelated.

Resource flexibility and capacity are thus important, as they determine what similarities can be captured and to what extent they can be exploited in terms of resource sharing. A high degree of flexibility reduces the need for certain similarities among activities with reference to the shared resources. Moreover, the existence of certain similarities may be captured in order to change or develop the resources activated by the activities. For instance, if manual operations are similar in certain respects these might be replaced by automatic work stations. The effects of that change may include increased cost efficiency, a more fixed capacity and a reduction of the degree of flexibility.

TECHNICAL INTERDEPENDENCE

Apart from the interdependence among activities dealt with in previous sections, technical interdependence among resources can be identified. From the perspective of an activity structure, resources can be seen as having two sides, one as products (being the results of activities), and the other as activated resources. Certain technical interdependence is directly associated with the vertical and horizontal interdependence of activities in activity structures. For instance, a set of components assembled or welded together must fit, and the activated resources and the products resulting from an activity must fit, e.g., the technical properties of an injection moulded plastic component are dependent on the mould activated in its production. Technical interdependence of this kind is quite obvious and is embedded in the activity structure as such. However, technical interdependence is seldom constrained to mere consequences of the vertical interdependence forming the activity structure, or to the connections between the result of a particular activity and the resources activated by it. Technical interdependence also cuts across activity structures in many different ways which cannot be derived from, or explained by, the activity structure itself.

Technical interdependence may be related to different technical dimensions such as physical attributes (shape), power, flows, strength, tolerances, vibration, and temperature. In addition, with regard to change, products' adaptability vis-à-vis one another may vary in terms of the different technical dimensions and also in the different contexts, or activity structures, to which they belong.

During product development certain delimited technical systems are in focus. How these are eventually designed impacts on how the activities needed to produce them may be organised. For instance, although certain considerations regarding the activity structure may be taken into account during the development process, the complexity within a technical system may constrain the possibilities of comprising similarity aspects.

To analyse technical interdependence within a particular technical system we may distinguish custom designed, or specific, products from standardised products, and identify the nature of their technical interdependence. As a consequence of the distinction between specific and standardised products, the interdependence may either be mutual or unilateral in terms of their adaptability vis-à-vis one another (see Figure 4.2). In addition, from the perspective of a certain firm (as a user) standardised products may be externally adapted or adaptable, such as standardised screws and nuts.

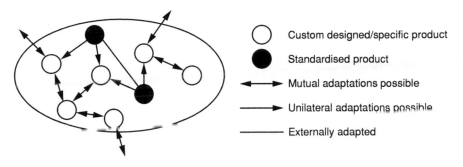

Custom designed/specific product

Standardised product

Mutual adaptations possible

Unilateral adaptations possible

Externally adapted

Figure 4.2 Standardised and custom designed/specific products

As a starting point for further exploration of the effects of technical interdependence, an example is given below describing how the technical interdependence in a technical system may be dealt with.

Three products (A, B and C in Figure 4.3), viewed by a firm who used them as components of its end product, had to fit together. This was problematic for several reasons. The tolerances were the basic technical dimension in this case, and were complicated because the three products consisted of different materials. All three products were end product specific and their adaptability depended on their connections to other products. The connections shown in Figure 4.3 are related to the particular technical dimension – tolerances – and, thus, to the problem in focus.

Product A was a plastic component produced in an injection moulding machine (F) in which a custom designed tool (E) was used. The plastic material chosen (D) and the machine affected the design of the tool and thus, indirectly, also some properties of product A. Furthermore, the plastic material directly affected the tolerances of product A. Product B was a cast component consisting of a standardised casting material (I) shaped by a tool (H). Product C was a component consisting basically of a bent steel plate. Product C had to fit to component G, which was a standardised component.

The conditions for adjusting any of the three components in focus (products A, B and C) differed, depending on their connections to the other products. A different choice of plastic material used to produce component A could be made in order to solve the problem, which could affect the choice of machine used. Changing the choice of material in component B would not solve the problem. Rather, a different design of the component, which would naturally affect the design of the tool (H) used, could solve the problem but would also impact on other related products than the two in focus. Moreover, a change in design of component B would affect other technical dimensions, such as technical stability

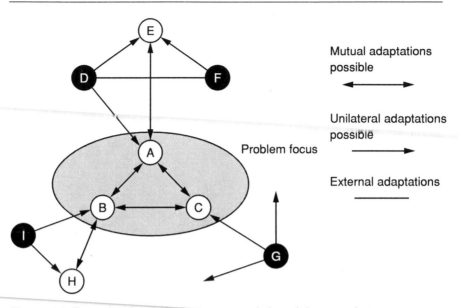

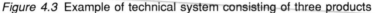

Figure 4.3 Example of technical system consisting of three products

and strength. Finally, component C could not be adjusted because of the connection to the standardised component (G). Component G could not be replaced by another standardised product without extensive impact on other technical dimensions related to power, speed and so on, affecting a large number of indirectly connected components. Thus, the alternative adjustments of the three products impacted in different ways, directly and indirectly, on related components and technical dimensions, owing to the technical interdependence among them.

This example shows how a rather limited problem, at first sight involving three interadjustable components, turns out to be complex, with direct and indirect impacts on several technical dimensions and products. The example illustrates some of the considerations involved in the discussions around how to handle the technical interdependence within a limited part of a larger technical system. Nevertheless, in the example, the technical interdependence is well known, as opposed to what is usually the case in product development projects wherein many technical connections (in terms of technical interdependence and technical dimensions) are discovered as the work progresses. Hence, most often technical considerations comprise a much higher degree of complexity. Moreover, during the development process the production of, for instance, the tools in the example may require a great deal of time. This affects further development efforts since after a certain point in time the tools may have to be dealt with as 'fixed', similar to the standardised components.

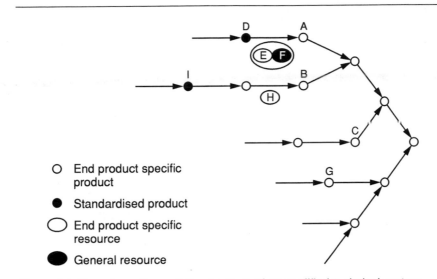

Figure 4.4 Transformation activity structure of exemplified technical system

If we consider a technical system in the light of the activity structure the technical interdependence may cut across it in different ways. The activity structure to which the technical system discussed above is connected may, for instance, be organised as illustrated in Figure 4.4 if we focus on the transformation activities only.

In principle, we may identify three categories of technical interdependence in terms of how it cuts across the activity structure.

First, there may be technical interdependence between products in the activity structure (see A in Figure 4.5). This category of interdependence may be exemplified by the technical performance (power) of the hydraulic unit in the hydraulic system case, to which certain other components within the T2–truck had to be adjusted. Another example was provided by the steering arm case where certain technical performance parameters could not be tested until the complete truck had been assembled. That is, technical interdependence prevailed among a number of components resulting from activities organised at different 'locations' in the activity structure.

Second, there may be technical interdependence between a product and a resource activated by another activity (see B in Figure 4.5). This can be exemplified by the moulds activated in the production of components in the steering arm case which had to fit components belonging to other part systems. The technical dimensions focused in this case were strength and fitting of holes.

Third, there may be technical interdependence between resources activated to produce different components in an end product related activity

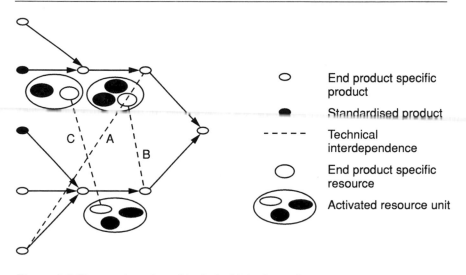

Figure 4.5 Three categories of technical interdependence

structure (see C in Figure 4.5). This may be exemplified by two moulds which must be interadjusted for the components produced by them to fit. Also, if painting of different components is undertaken by different subcontractors, or the painting activates different painting facilities for other reasons, the equipment must be interadjusted to make the result of the painting activities look the same. The two latter examples, where resources are subject to technical interdependence to other products and resources in a particular end product related activity structure, imply different connections between end product related activity structures since the individual resources are also the results of such structures.

Let us now return to the exemplified technical system and consider the firms involved. We get different pictures when focusing on the technical system compared to when focusing on the activity structure. First, the picture of the firms involved in the technical system would be as in Figure 4.6.

All three components were produced by different suppliers and therefore any adjustments would require involvement of the suppliers, or alternatively entail a change of supplier (if, for instance, a change of material in product A had been needed). The tools used in the production of components A and B were produced and adjusted by tool suppliers, and, hence, any change affecting the tools would necessarily involve them.

However, when focusing on how the activities are organised among the firms involved the picture may be different (see Figure 4.7).

The connection between (a) the way the activities are organised among firms, and (b) the way the technical system(s) is/are dealt with by the

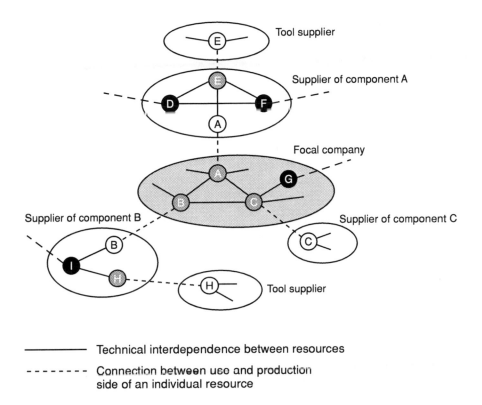

Technical interdependence between resources

 Connection between use and production
side of an individual resource

Figure 4.6 Firms involved in technical system

firms is not obvious. Furthermore, there are numerous different alternatives associated with both. Therefore, when activities are reorganised the responsibilities for the technical system(s) of concern need be dealt with as related issues in their own right. For instance, where out-sourcing of transformation activities is concerned, the responsibility for the technical system can be dealt with in two ways, in principle. It can be either kept in-house, which implies that subcontracting is applied, or out-sourced along with the production activities. In the latter case 'function' or 'black-box' purchasing is applied. Neither alternative is, however, clear cut, as there are numerous alternative approaches to both.

To summarise, the technical interdependence among products and resources incorporated in activity structures cuts across them in different ways. The way technical interdependence is taken care of by the firms involved may take on different patterns which are not static or self-evident. There may be certain trade-offs between, on the one hand, creating and

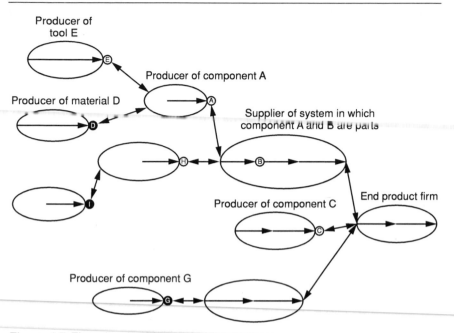

Figure 4.7 Firms involved in activity structure

capturing of similarities to make the activity structure efficient and, on the other, integrating the technical system(s) to achieve 'the right' performance characteristics. In addition, the considerations are related to how other activity structures are organised, and how other technical systems are designed. Hence, the complexity characterising activity structures is immense when taking technical interdependence into consideration, since there are always numerous sources of concerns when organising activities. We next look into the firms working in this complex structure.

THE FIRM AS A 'POOL' OF RESOURCES AND A 'SWITCHBOARD' FOR ACTIVITIES

The firm may be characterised as a 'pool' or a 'bundle' of resources (Penrose 1959) activated by a unique set of activities. Seen in the context of a larger activity structure in which the firm is involved, the firm can be regarded as a 'node', or as a 'switchboard', wherein a certain number of activity chains directed to different customers are connected.

In Figure 4.8, an example of the activities organised within a firm is shown. Three activity chains (A, B and C) which are parts in three different end product related activity structures are organised within the firm. As a 'switchboard' in the activity structure every firm somehow connects the activity chains organised within it.

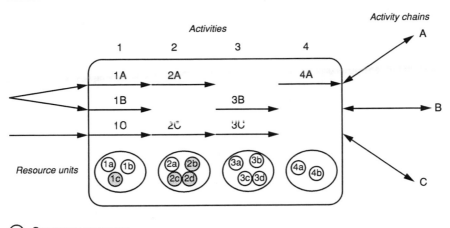

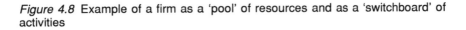

○ Common resource

◑ Resource specific to a
particular end product

Figure 4.8 Example of a firm as a 'pool' of resources and as a 'switchboard' of
activities

Activity 1, which is needed in all three activity chains organised in the
firm, activates a resource unit consisting of three resources (1a, 1b and
1c). Suppose that resources 1a and 1b are common and shared among the
three activity chains, while resource 1c is only activated by 1B, since it is
specific to activity chain B. For instance, the shared resources may be
personnel and equipment while the specific resource may be a tool, a
fixture or the like which is specific to a certain end product related activity
structure in which activity chain B is a part.

Activity 2, undertaken by the firm in activity chains A and C, activates
a resource unit consisting of four resources. Of these only one, 2a, is
common and shared by the activities (2A and 2C) while resources 2b and
2c are only activated by activity 2A, and resource 2d is activated only by
activity 2C.

Activity 3 is needed within activity chains B and C, and activates a
resource unit consisting of four resources, all of which are common to both
activities, although some of them may need adjustments specific to the
respective activity chain. Activity 4 is only part of activity chain A, and
the resources activated by it are therefore, at least at the moment, not
shared by any other activity. Furthermore, activity chains A and B require
common input, while different input is required in activity chain C.

Now if we consider the efficiency of the way the activities are organised,
capacity utilisation alone is not enough for the firm to be efficient with regard
to the larger activity structure. First, the more the individual activities within

each one of the activity chains organised within the firm are interconnected horizontally, i.e., through resource sharing (on the activity level), the more efficient and difficult to replace is the firm for its individual customers. Secondly, the more adapted to the needs of each of its customers, the more efficient is the firm. Rather than maximising one of these aspects above the other, the overall efficiency of the firm is determined by its ability to combine these two aspects. And, although this may be a balancing act, it is not basically a matter of optimising the two.

Obviously, interdependence of various kinds among activities puts constraints upon what can be done by individual firms as their activities are connected to those of others in many ways. At the same time, interdependence constitutes the foundation on which the firm exists and as such it is always the starting point for its future development of activities and resources.

A good example of firms succeeding in dealing with vertical, horizontal and technical interdependence is the supplier of hydraulic systems – HP – and its supplier – the producer of hydraulic units. The latter had replaced various disparate activity chains resulting in different hydraulic systems within previously separate end product related activity structures into one activity chain, resulting in a standardised hydraulic unit. This activity chain thus became part of several end product related activity structures. Similarities in certain important technical dimensions had been taken advantage of while other well defined technical properties had been left to adjustments in order to make the hydraulic units fit the different end products. The result for the customers was not only cost efficiency but also better technical performance. Identification of similarities among activities or chains of activities in different activity structures may therefore not only be exploited as cost reductions through efficient resource utilisation or resource development, but also as a means of creating value, as in this case improved technical performance. The customers' abilities and willingness to make the necessary technical adjustments for the standardised system to fit into their end products may depend on how activity interdependence can be taken care of in their respective activity structures. In addition, HP played an important role by acting as a 'switch-board' between the activities undertaken by its suppliers and of its customers.

As a 'pool' of resources, the use of which are not given, the firm may develop its resources and/or its use of them in different ways and directions. However, the development is always related to the prior state. For instance, adaptation of one or several activities can make it possible to share a certain resource unit among them instead of activating different ones. If, for instance, activities 3 and 4 in the example shown in Figure 4.8 are similar with reference to fulfilling similar functions, this may be exploited so that they activate the same resource unit instead. However, this may require adjustments of one or several of the activities. Assume, for instance, that activity 3 is spot welding and activity 4 upset riveting. If the customer to which activity chain A is directed can be persuaded to accept spot welding instead of riveting, the three activity chains may all activate the welding resource unit, which may be advantageous for all parties involved. However, this may require adjustments of other activities undertaken by the customer to which the altered activity chain is directed.

Developments in the opposite direction may also increase efficiency. For instance, the individual activities activating a common resource may be more efficiently undertaken if they are instead undertaken as two activities activating two different resource units. Reasons for this development may be a combination of scarce capacity and different requirements on the result of the activity (for instance painting with ordinary and two component paint which represent considerable differences in cost as well as painting quality). Hence, both cost and value reasons may underlie a change of this kind.

Horizontal interdependence has hitherto only concerned the production or transformation activities of the firm. In addition, similarities in terms of how different activity chains are co-ordinated by the firm affect its performance as a 'switchboard'. Four categories of similarity with regard to activity chain co-ordination can be identified:

1 internally within the firm
2 between the firm and its customers
3 between the firm and its suppliers
4 in the connections between the firm's customers and suppliers

These four dimensions of activity chains are illustrated in Figure 4.9.

First, the activity chains organised in a firm may be similar in terms of the sequence of activities undertaken, i.e., the flow between the resource units may be more or less similar. The similarity among the different activity chains in this respect can be assumed to affect the extent of internal co-ordination. In the hydraulic system and the steering arm cases, the number of activities was low and the flows among the few resource units involved were similar. This can be contrasted against the complete fork carriage case and the machine body case in which there were many activated resource units and the flows among them were different. The machine body case can be seen as especially complex since not only internal resource units were activated by the system supplier, but also various sub-suppliers' resource units.

Second, the co-ordination of activities between a firm and its customers may be more or less similar depending on the links between the activities undertaken by the firm and the activities undertaken by the different customers. If these links are similar, the co-ordination activities needed to make them work may be facilitated. In the hydraulic system case there

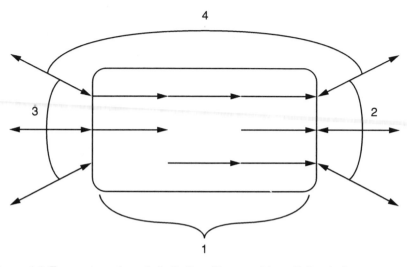

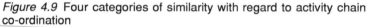

Figure 4.9 Four categories of similarity with regard to activity chain co-ordination

were obvious similarities in this respect since the links among the activities undertaken by the hydraulic unit producer and by HP, both co-ordinated by HP, were similar with reference to the customers' assembly activities undertaken thereafter. Therefore, the customers' requirements regarding delivery, quality, etc. were similar as they were equally sensitive to disturbances in their production. Hence, if the links are similar there may be similarities to be taken advantage of in the exchange activities.

Third, similarities in the co-ordination of activities between the firm and its suppliers can be of two kinds:

1 The activity links between the firm and the suppliers, or different supplier categories (e.g., suppliers of customised and standardised products), may be more or less similar.
2 The supplier relationships may be shared if there is a high degree of similarity with reference to the customers' needs of certain materials and components.

In the hydraulic system case there were interesting similarities with reference to the producer of the hydraulic units and the way HP could handle the connections between this supplier and its system customers. These connections were important for the customers, especially when designing new or modified products. With all system customers but SweFork, the relationships to suppliers of additional components could be shared. SweFork chose not to benefit from these similarities since there were similarities to be taken advantage of within its own boundaries. Since the same additional component suppliers could be used for its various truck models, similarities in activities related to purchasing as well as to service and spare parts handling could be taken advantage of.

In the steering arm case, several components were specific to the steering arm irrespective of whether they were assembled by SweFork or the system supplier. Hence, the degree of similarity in the purchasing of components was low regardless of who took care of it. However, some components were common to other end products assembled by SweFork, who therefore wanted to maintain its relationships with those suppliers.

In the complete fork carriage case and the machine body case, the similarities seemed to be high in terms of suppliers used, enabling the system suppliers to share their supplier relationships among several activity chains directed to their different customers. Moreover, in the machine body case, the discussion around how to handle the replacement of specific format steel plate resulting in a choice of standard steel plate illustrates how similarities can be created and used by a firm which is aware of the relation between similarity and efficiency.

Fourth, if there are specific connections between the customer and supplier relationships, there may be similarities in these connections and, thus, in the way these connections can be co-ordinated by the firm. For instance, if the customers of a firm require different brands of a certain component, there may be similarities to be taken advantage of in the way the supplier relationships, although specific to the individual customers, can be handled.

Nevertheless, as for transformation activities, creation of similarities is not always the best way for the firm to be efficient vis-à-vis individual counterparts. Counterpart specific solutions may be needed since their value for the counterpart may exceed the costs of not taking advantage of economies of scale.

To summarise, the firm may be characterised as a 'pool' of resources and as a 'switchboard' of activities. The ways in which the resources are activated are not given and change over time. However, each firm can be assumed to be activating its 'pool' of resources to the best of its ability to be efficient. The efficiency of the firm, in turn, is a matter of (a) creating and capturing similarities among the activities organised within its boundary, and, (b) adapting its activities and resources to the needs of its customers.

CONSEQUENCES OF INTERDEPENDENCE IN ACTIVITY STRUCTURES

Firms are usually regarded as independent of one another. As independent actors they are free to choose suppliers. Consequently, their customers are free to choose whatever suppliers they please. For independent firms, there are effects of these choices on aggregate volumes in purchasing, production and sales. Here, we have seen interdependent firms and the co-ordination required of their activities to make the activity structures they are involved in work. We have argued, in contrast to the description of independent firms, that the interdependence among firms is not only an empirical fact, but also a consequence of efficient ways of organising activities and resources among them. Hence, the relationships between firms needed in order to co ordinate their activities cannot be regarded as market failures. Interdependence, however, entails complexity, owing to the way it cuts across formal firm boundaries. This complexity is dealt with by firms.

Taking interdependence into account, however, the firm is confronted with a number of specific considerations. As actors in activity structures firms always strive to optimise their own parts within it. When trying to optimise its activities and resources, each firm must decide which counterparts it is prepared to adjust to. Each and every such choice impacts on the interdependence of the firm's activities and resources. There are three reasons why this is problematic.

First, there are always conflicting concerns, not least when technical systems are developed and the activities needed to produce them are organised. Thus, instead of trying to find optima, compromises must be sought. This, in turn, redirects the focus from how activities and resources can be most efficiently organised towards how the firms involved interact with each other. Clearly, it is through interaction that compromises are created.

Second, the complexity of an activity structure owing to interdependence makes it impossible for anyone to fully grasp it. Therefore, simplifications are needed. This entails neglecting to utilise certain efficiency potentials. For instance, a purchasing policy decision forcing the engineers to use a certain number of existing components will impact positively on production efficiency and reduce the development costs of the firm, but at the same time it limits the potential for the engineers to create or discover new combinations which could have been valuable for the customers.

Third, activity structures are always both the subject and the cause of change. All kinds of imbalances, resulting from the fact that activity structures are never optimised, are one of the main sources of change, and since there are always an abundance of interdependence aspects to be considered, firms must choose which interdependence aspects, and thus counterparts, they are prepared to adjust to when organising their activities. The direction of these efforts affects the compromises they reach when interacting with their counterparts. In the next chapter, we identify certain boundaries within activity structures with an influence on the interaction between firms and thus on their joint abilities to compromise.

Chapter 5

Boundaries in activity structures

To be efficient firms need (a) to utilise their resources, and (b) to adapt their activities and resources to their counterparts. The way activities are divided and organised among firms affects how they deal with these two interrelated issues. This, in turn, impacts on each firm's individual efficiency as well as the efficiency of the whole activity structure. When the activities and resources of firms are interdependent there are other boundaries than the actual, or formal, firm boundaries that also require attention. These can be seen as consequences of the interdependence among firms.

First, a boundary between general and specific activities with reference to a particular end product can be identified. This boundary thus relates the activities that are specifically adapted to the end product to those that are not. It is important since it is within the specific part of the end product related activity structure that the activities must be specifically related to other activities in order to be carried out efficiently.

Second, from a particular firm's perspective, an awareness boundary can be identified in the activity structure based on what individuals, and groups of individuals, know about activities undertaken by other firms in the activity structures the firm is involved in. Awareness of activities undertaken by other firms constitutes a basis for interaction with them, and at the same time it is through interaction that the individual firm's awareness boundary can be extended. Consequently, for the interaction to take place and be fruitful, other firms' awareness of the activities undertaken by the firm is of equal importance.

Third, as a result of interdependence, activities are always subject to joint influence from several firms. Therefore, no individual firm can act independently when organising its activities. This may be seen as problematic since the firm cannot fully control the activities organised within its own formal boundaries. Overlapping influence boundaries can thus be identified in the activity structure. Hence, while each firm influences other firms' activities and resources it is influenced by other firms.

GENERAL *VERSUS* SPECIFIC ACTIVITIES

We begin by focusing on the end product related activity structures that have been used here as a means of delimiting part of a wider activity structure. The individual activities in an end product related activity structure can be characterised either as general or specific to the end product. This is one of the main differences among the activities needed to produce the end product. General activities result in standardised products which may be used for various purposes by different users. Specific activities result in products specific to an end product and can therefore only be part of that particular end product related activity structure. However, the activated resources need not be specific to the activity, or its result of it, to be so. Prior to the start of a chain of end product specific activities, there is always some standardised product or material.

An end product related activity structure can be divided into a general and a specific part as shown in Figure 5.1. At the point where an activity chain turns from general to specific, the complementary activities become closely complementary, using Richardson's (1972) categorisation of activities. Therefore, the conditions for co-ordination of the activities differ. Standardised products resulting from the general activities at the general-specific boundary may be subject to market exchange while the specific activities need to be co-ordinated either by relationship exchange or through internal direction, i.e., taken care of within the end product firm.

For the individual firm the general-specific boundary is concerned with matters of choosing standardised products. Using a standardised product implies that the technical interdependence between the individual standardised product and the specific products to which it is connected is unilateral. Specific products, on the other hand, may be regarded as mutually dependent and, thus, mutually adaptable, to some extent. Hence, the technical interdependence has to be handled differently since the specific products that are used in combination with the standardised ones have to be adjusted to make them fit if no better fitting standardised product is available. In contrast, two specific products may be regarded as inter-adjustable even when certain dimensions of one or both of them may be difficult to adjust.

In the hydraulic system case, the standardised hydraulic units were adapted to suit the end products of HP's system customers. The last general activity was the production of hydraulic units, and the first specific activity in the chain was the end product specific adjustments of the hydraulic units. Both these activities were undertaken by the producer of hydraulic units, and were followed by assembly, undertaken by HP.

In the steering arm case, some of the components used were standardised (i.e., resulting from general activities), while others, such as the

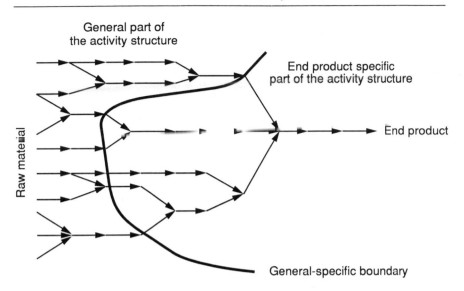

Figure 5.1 Boundary between general and specific activities in an end product related activity structure

injection moulded plastic components, were specific to the steering arm in the T2–truck. The processing of plastic raw materials can thus be regarded as the last general activity in the activity chains, resulting in the plastic components which were to be assembled into the steering arm.

In the complete fork carriage case, the activity chain turned from general to specific by the machining activities carried out by the potential system supplier. This firm was buying standardised steel products which were transformed by the various machining activities into components and systems specific to the customers' end products.

The boundary between general and specific activities in the activity structure resulting in the T2–truck before and after the (intended) change from component to system sourcing is shown in Figure 5.2.

Figure 5.2 shows the main consequences of the changes in relation to SweFork's firm boundary and to the general-specific boundary. While SweFork's pre-assembly activities and all the related exchange activities decrease, the extent of activities undertaken within the end product specific activity structure outside the firm increases. As a result, the end product specific activities undertaken by suppliers become associated with other activities organised within their boundaries. Thereby, the efficiency with which each one of these activities can be performed becomes dependent upon the other activities undertaken by the suppliers and, consequently, on the resource sharing that can be obtained by them. The extent to which there were real similarities to be utilised by and within the suppliers,

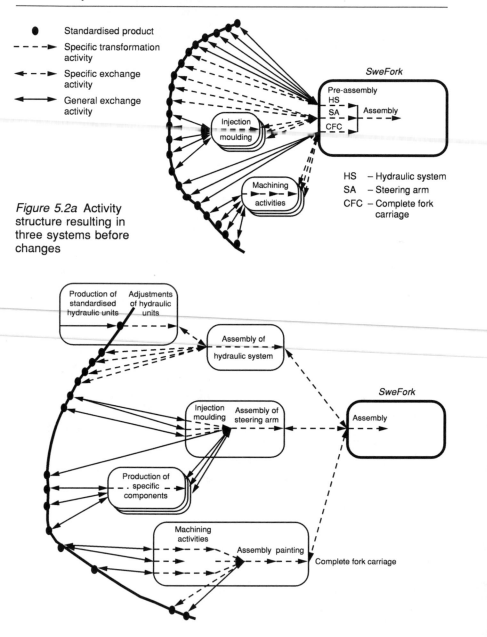

Standardised product

Specific transformation activity

Specific exchange activity

General exchange activity

SweFork

Pre-assembly
HS
SA   Assembly
CFC

HS – Hydraulic system
SA – Steering arm
CFC – Complete fork carriage

Injection moulding

Machining activities

Figure 5.2a Activity structure resulting in three systems before changes

Production of standardised hydraulic units   Adjustments of hydraulic units

Assembly of hydraulic system

SweFork

Injection moulding   Assembly of steering arm

Assembly

Production of specific components

Machining activities

Assembly painting

Complete fork carriage

Figure 5.2b Activity structure after changes

enabling them to perform the activities more efficiently than SweFork, varied among the cases.

In order to change an activity structure, like the one illustrated in Figure 5.2, one important requirement is that there actually are similarities to be taken advantage of outside the firm. Hence, the actors involved in an activity structure organise and develop their activities in their own best interests, but cannot do this independently of how other actors organise and develop their activities. The ways in which the actors develop their parts of the activity structure are therefore partly reactions to how their counterparts and third parties, such as their suppliers' other customers, develop theirs. Thus, the current direction of the dynamics within activity structures, reflected on an aggregated level in decreasing degrees of vertical integration, may be towards organising an increasing number of specific activities beyond the firm boundary. This requires, but at the same time also creates, similarities to be captured. In two of the cases presented, the importance of how Volvo and Scania had organised their activity structures was obvious, as SweFork could benefit from similarities among activities undertaken by shared suppliers.

In the machine body case, the activity chain resulting in machine bodies was organised differently during three identified phases. The differences concerned the nature of the activities themselves, how the activities were divided among the firms and the extent of general *versus* specific transformation activities in the chain (see Figure 5.3).

In the first phase standardised steel plates were used by the machining firm which then undertook three specific activities: cutting, drilling and bending. Thereafter, SweFork performed four specific activities prior to the truck's completion. In the second phase the system supplier – Systech – undertook two machine body specific activities; machining and welding. Furthermore, Systech organised two additional specific activities at other firms. A steel works produced special format steel plate purchased by Systech, and a painting firm painted the welded machine bodies. Hence, three firms undertook machine body specific activities before SweFork refined them further into complete trucks. In the third phase the activities were at first characterised as in phase two. The reorganisation among the firms shortened the specific activity chain undertaken outside SweFork both in terms of number of specific activities (from four to one) and firms (from three to one). Furthermore, when the special format steel plate had to be replaced by standard format plate, owing to volume and time interdependence, the specific part of the activity chain was shortened.

The boundary between general and specific activities is important since it sets the terms for the extent of the specific part of the end product activity structure. This, in turn, is of importance as it is within this part of the activity structure that similarities to other activity structures need to be captured which thus affect its efficiency. Hence, for the end product

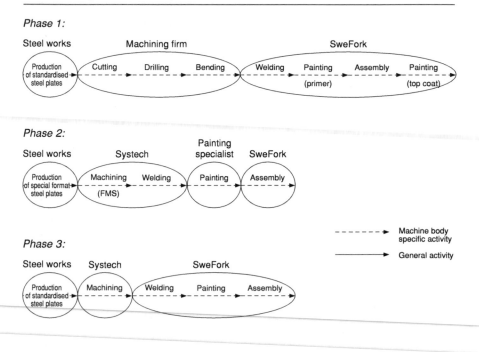

Figure 5.3 Activity chains resulting in machine bodies during three phases

firm it is important to be aware of the interdependence to which the end product specific activities are subjected. In addition, the choice of standardised products affects the activities refining them further, as well as the possibilities of combining them with other standardised and specific products within the activity structure.

AWARENESS AND INTERACTION

Individuals and/or groups of individuals within the end product firm may be more or less aware of the activities and their interdependence within the end product related activity structure. Where complex end products such as trucks and cars are concerned, no individual is able to be aware of the whole activity structure. In many cases not even the full range of activities undertaken by his or her 'own' firm can possibly be within the scope of any individual's awareness. Therefore, awareness about activities and resources related to a certain end product, and the relevant connections these may have to other end product related structures, can be assumed to be subject to joint efforts among several individuals and/or groups. Their ability to jointly utilise their respective fragments of awareness to create relevant pictures of the complex contest they act in is thereby decisive to a particular firm's awareness boundary in the activity structure of concern. This, in turn, affects the behaviour of the firm.

Lack of awareness of how the end product specific activities are organised outside the firm may cause unexpected problems. One example is found in the machine body case where the reduction in production volume in phase three resulted in problems, owing to time and volume interdependence in the way the activities had been organised by Systech. These problems might have been handled differently if SweFork had been aware of how the activities were organised and of their interdependence.

Obviously, awareness about activities and resources, and most importantly the interdependence among them, affects firms' possibilities to increase the efficiency of their activity structures over time. However, this not only concerns the possibilities to better exploit resources by capturing similarities. The possibilities of identifying and creating new resource combinations, i.e., of innovation, are also deeply affected by the awareness boundaries of individuals and firms. Naturally, it is only within the existing scope of awareness new combinations can be found. Moreover, when new combinations are created the interdependence among activities and resources are restructured which, in turn, may impact on the awareness boundaries of the firm.

In order for the firm to be able to identify and capture efficiency potentials in terms of similarities in the specific part of the activity structure outside the firm, a certain awareness of the other activities and activity chains handled by the suppliers is needed. This awareness may include the suppliers' other customers and their activities, i.e., the other activity chains to which the activity chains directed to the firm are, or may become, connected. But one firm's awareness of others' activities and resources is not sufficient to find efficient ways of organising activities and combining resources vis-à-vis its counterparts. Rather, overlapping awareness boundaries are needed for firms to create better solutions. Through interaction they can combine their respective knowledge of how a certain product is produced, refined and consumed. Thereby, the product's different contexts can be analysed jointly by the firms. This, in turn, may provide grounds for developing it further. Hence, a certain awareness of the counterparts' activities and resources is needed for fruitful interaction to take place.

Obviously, these aspects of awareness are closely related to learning (Bångens 1997) as the awareness boundary seems to be decisive to firms' possibilities of finding new activity and resource combinations. Hence, the more two counterparts' awareness boundaries overlap the better are their possibilities of interacting and thereby jointly finding new and better ways to relate their activities and resources.

An extension of the awareness over the general-specific boundary may entail recognition of potential advantages of making adaptations and thus turning certain general activities into specific ones. The result would then be an extension of the specific part of the end product related activity structure.

INFLUENCE AND INTERACTION

Traditionally, firms are assumed to control resources through ownership. Moreover, this control is supposed to impact positively on the firm's efficiency since by maintaining control over its resources the firm is free to choose how to use them. Thus, the firm is supposed to be able to design and organise its activities independently. However, we have seen above that firms' activities are interdependent as a result of efficient ways to organise their activities. When interdependence prevails, resource control is not a prerequisite for firms to be efficient. Instead, the question of how the activities activating the resources are designed and are related to other firms' activities gains importance. Hence, the design and organisation of activities is not based on resource control but on activity interdependence. Therefore, instead of focusing on resource control, the way the firm influences other firms' activities and the way these, in turn, influence the activities performed by the firm comes into focus. Resources thus take on a new role for the firm, especially the way resources can be used to influence other firms' resources and activities. Another aspect of equal importance is the way the counterparts' resources influence the firm's own resources. This mutuality needs be underlined since it makes this picture very different from the traditional view of the role of resources.

Firms may use different means to influence other firms' activities. Based on the foregoing section, awareness and interaction seem to be the best way of finding compromises that are efficient for the individual firms as well as for the whole activity structure. Yet large, powerful firms may exercise influence over their suppliers' activities based on their power and not on mutuality and interaction. This may result in undesired long-term structural effects attributable to efficiency losses resulting from the suppliers' inability to develop and utilise similarities among the needs of their powerful customers and other current or potential customers. Naturally, these efficiency losses not only affect the suppliers but also their customers. In addition, in striving to maintain control, the powerful customers may also consciously limit their suppliers' awareness of their resources and activities, with further negative impact on the suppliers' possibilities to contribute to better technical solutions and/or more efficient ways of producing them.

In the SweFork case this type of effect resulted from the fact that the suppliers were previously only involved at a late stage when new trucks were developed. This made it difficult for them to develop and utilise similarities among the activities performed by them in relation to their different customers.

One short example may further illustrate the causes and effects of disregarding the importance of awareness and joint influence when organising activities. A firm was developing a technical system of great importance for the technical performance of its end product. One component within this technical system was developed jointly with a supplier. This supplier was a specialist for this kind of component and had several of the world's largest and most demanding customers in the field. When developing the technical system the customer perceived it as important not to give the supplier insights into any other connected components or the technical context of the system since confidentiality was considered of utmost importance. This resulted in the supplier suggesting a large number of technical solutions that did not really fit into the technical system. The customer realised why this was, but could not specify the requirements for the component in such a way that the supplier could develop it independently. The customer did not know the technology of the component, and the supplier was not allowed to participate in the testing of how the component worked together with the other components in the system. The engineers working at the customer firm did not know anything about how components of this kind were produced by the supplier. The supplier produced around a million customised components a year for its different customers, and had been able to develop fully automated lines in which customisation of the components could be made at the same time as very high production efficiency could be maintained.

In the end, after a number of suggested technical solutions, tests and failures, the firms agreed on a solution which was not technically superior to the ones already performed by the supplier for its other customers. Furthermore, the design of this component made it impossible for the supplier to produce it in the fully automated lines. Instead, it was manually assembled in a corner of the factory. The production volumes were about 20,000 a year, and to develop automated production solutions with higher efficiency and lower failure rates approximately half a million items were required. Consequently, the price for the components was more than twice the price paid by the supplier's other customers.

This example illustrates that although the two firms interacted during the development process, the limited awareness of the counterpart's resources and activities affected their possibilities (especially the supplier's) to influence. Potentially, the firm and its supplier could have jointly reached a solution with high technical performance and high production efficiency, but only on the condition that they also permitted mutual accessibility beyond each others' boundaries.

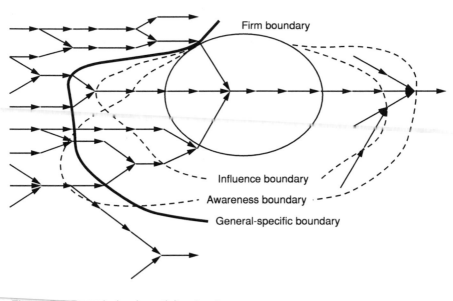

Figure 5.4 Boundaries in activity structures

THE FIRM AND ITS BOUNDARIES IN THE ACTIVITY STRUCTURE

Three boundaries in activity structures have been identified and are illustrated in Figure 5.4. The general-specific boundary is related to the end product and relates the activities that are specific to the end product to those that are not. The awareness boundary is related to individuals' joint knowledge about the activities undertaken outside the firm. The influence boundary concerns the extent to which a firm influences the activities in the activity structure in which it is involved.

The 'actual' firm boundary, i.e., the boundary around the activities actually undertaken by the firm, must always be seen in the light of the other boundaries in the activity structure in which the firm is involved. If this firm boundary is regarded as in a firm-market context it is assumed to separate the firm's own activities from those of other firms. Interdependent activities are thus supposed to be organised within the firm boundary, while activities undertaken by other firms are assumed to be independent of the firm's own. In contrast, when the activities undertaken by different firms are interdependent, the firm boundary relates rather than separates the activities performed within it with those organised 'outside' it. The identified boundaries are consequences of the interdependence among firms and it is important to understanding how activities are and can be related. The more the firm is aware of activities undertaken outside its boundary the better its possibilities to relate to them and, consequently, the better the counterparts' awareness of the firm's activities the better are their possibilities to relate to them. In addition, every firm whose activities are subject to interdependence is also subject to other firms' influence on how its activities are designed and organised. At the same time the firm also has some influence on the activities performed by others.

Chapter 6

The dynamics of activity structures

ACTIVITY STRUCTURES COMING TO LIFE

In this book a static model explaining efficiency in industrial systems has been developed, illustrated and discussed. It is important to emphasise that the model is static since it cannot be used to explain or predict change in industrial systems. However, activity structures are characterised by their dynamic nature, or the 'life' in them. Thus, the model can explain the efficiency in the organisation of *given* activities among *given* firms activating *given* resources. Yet the dynamics in industrial systems is not about division of given activities and resources but about the creation of activities and resources which are not given at all. The creation of new resources and activities, in turn, is always basically a matter of new combinations (Penrose 1959).

One possible reaction to the fact that the model is entirely static is to regard this as a shortcoming. However, the model is obviously empirically relevant since it can be applied to explain the efficiency of alternative ways of organising activities. Hence, there is not necessarily something wrong with the model, but rather with *the logic* underlying all models of this kind. This logic rests on the basic assumption that there are certain situational conditions (here based on complementarity and similarity), characterising activities and the ways they activate resources, connected to certain appropriate forms of co-ordination. Efficient co-ordination is the main objective, and there is a causal link between the conditions associated with the situation and the proper forms of co-ordination. But when relationships are used as a means of co-ordinating activities, more than co-ordination comes out of them. This is because relationships entail 'life' in industrial systems. This 'life' springs from the interaction between firms which entails changes in the conditions characterising the activities subject to co-ordination and the resources activated. There may be certain conditions based on which a relationship is 'chosen' as a means of co-ordinating certain activities, but once the parties have become involved in a relationship the conditions may become subject to changes resulting from identification of new resource and activity combinations. Thereby, relationships as a form of co-ordination differ distinctively from market exchanges and internally directed co-ordination. That is, neither firms, activities nor resources can be regarded as 'givens' when firms interact. If we maintain the focus on the activity dimension, the similarities that are developed and captured, and the adjustments (close complementarity among the counterparts' activities just implies *that there are adjustments*) made may all change through the interaction between the parties involved in a relationship. So while market exchange is determined by what is exchanged, the adjustments of activities and resources, which may necessitate relationship co-ordination in the first place, may take on new forms within the frame of a relationship.

We have thus stated that the static division of labour model can explain why organising given activities in a particular way is more or less efficient than other ways of organising them. However, when relationships coordinate activities there is more to it than mere co-ordination. Over time, activities and resources other than those initially subjected to interdependence become subject to 'confrontation' when a relationship has been established. These confrontations, effected through the interaction between the firms involved, give rise to possibilities of finding new combinations of activities and resources.

In the SweFork case there are several examples of how new resource and activity combinations sprang from relationships, although this was not 'intended'. In the fork carriage case the contemplated system supplier often suggested better solutions to its customers based on its knowledge of how the customers produced their end products. For instance, the supplier suggested that one customer use pressing instead of gas cutting and welding which would reduce costs and improve quality. The same supplier suggested that another customer use standardised profiles instead of cut and bent steel plate. To be able to make contributions of this kind the supplier needed to become involved early in development projects and to have some knowledge of the activities and resources performed and activated by the customer and/or other parties, e.g., the customer's other suppliers. For SweFork the supplier developed carriers to facilitate its internal transportation. These turned out to be useful also in facilitating external as well as internal transportation within SweFork's facilities. Extending the use of the carriers thus made transportation of the heavy fork carriages easier and also reduced the risk of damage. The supplier of fork carriages also contributed to the development of SweFork's assembly jigs, which made assembly time reductions possible. These are all examples of how relationships came to life, of how new ways of activating and combining resources were found through interaction.

In the machine body case, the 'matching' of resources was central and the production volume was one important factor determining the way the activities could be efficiently organised within and among the firms. Also, resource development entailed changes in the way the activities were organised over time. Interestingly, the case also illustrated how the relationship made certain problems subject to joint problem solving. This was reflected by the problematic effects of SweFork's reduced and less regular sales. Owing to the fact that SweFork was involved in a relationship with the system supplier and that this firm was involved in relationships with other parties, a number of alternative solutions to the problem could be identified. For instance, one of the possible solutions was that SweFork could use a particular standardised format steel plate that was stocked by the system supplier, since its other customers used them, to increase availability and thereby reduce lead time. The relationship with SweFork and with some of its other customers thus enabled the system supplier to suggest a solution based on the creation of similarities which, in turn, increased the time and volume flexibility in the way the activities were organised. Had SweFork carried out the activities in-house and thus bought the plates on its own, the volumes would not have been sufficiently large for this to be an efficient solution. The supplier's relationships with different suppliers such as a steel works and a distributor, and some of the customers requiring products which were similar in different respects, made this supplier able to suggest several alternative solutions to the problem. And, while SweFork would have had to replace one supplier with another, this turned out not to be necessary when the supplier's relationships could be activated.

The result of the 'life' that springs from relationships can not be predicted in advance, either in terms of what changes will take place at the activity 'level', or the structural effects of the changes on the industrial system 'level'. One interesting aspect of the dynamics, however, considering the 'life' springing from relationships, is transitions among co-ordination forms (Bångens and Dubois 1995). These transitions are particularly interesting when market exchange and internal direction is replaced by relationships. Market exchange may be replaced by relationship exchange when, for instance, a customer needs a custom specific variant of a standardised product which was previously subject to exchange. Or, other changes than production adjustments may proceed adaptations of the product subject to exchange, for instance, adjustments of a logistical nature which necessitate interaction between the firms. Through this interaction 'confrontations' giving rise to further adaptations may arise. When internal direction is replaced by relationship exchange this may be, as in the SweFork case, outsourcing of one or several activities to a supplier with which the firm is already involved in a relationship. This may be the result of interaction giving rise to new activity and resource combinations.

We now analyse an example where the structural results of both these transitions are combined. Consider two alternative ways of organising the

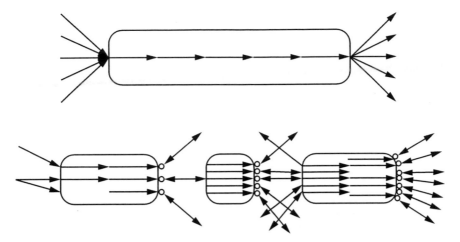

Figure 6.1 Two alternative ways of organising the same set of activities

same set of activities. The first is a highly vertically integrated firm whose exchange is mainly market based, the other is a situation in which several firms connected by relationships perform the same set of activities together (see Figure 6.1).

In the first case we may assume that the activities are subject to a high degree of efficiency owing to sufficient production volumes, i.e., that the resource capacity is fully utilised and economies of scale are exploited. If we look for sources from which new combinations may spring there are no obvious ones in the structure. The reason for this is the 'isolation' of the firm owing to the independence provided by market exchange. A similar argument is given by Penrose (1959: 86): 'no firm ever perceives the complete range of services [activities] available from any resource, because the range of services recognised is for the most part confined by the management's existing ideas as to the possible combinations.' Still, Penrose (1959: 56) assumes that changes may take place even in 'the absence of any change in external circumstances or in fundamental technological knowledge'. However, according to Penrose, the potential for innovation 'grows out of the firm's routine operations, just as Marshall's businessman finds the basis for his experiments in the results of his daily business'. In this latter reference the connection between the firm and its context seems to encompass more to Penrose than large numbers of faceless and independent counterparts being dealt with as aggregates, as the traditional conceptualisation of markets suggests.

Hence, even to the most creative manager the possibilities of finding new combinations internally within a structure 'isolated' by independence must soon be exhausted (cf. Lundvall (1988) arguing that the learning interface in vertically integrated systems becomes too narrow). Assuming there is independence between the firm and its counterparts, which by definition characterises market exchange, production volume increases are clearly what may trigger change in the vertically integrated structure. Growth, in turn, is complicated owing to the principle of non-proportional change (Boulding 1953), since each individual activity is featured differently in terms of imperfectly divisible resources.

If we instead consider the second way of organising the activities in Figure 6.1 we may first focus the need for a large enough volume for each individual activity to be carried out efficiently. However, in this activity structure the principle of non-proportional change does not cause problems in the same manner since the outputs of each specialising firm are specifically adapted to different counterparts. Thus, not only is it easier to achieve efficient resource utilisation (i.e., lower cost) in this structure, but it is also possible to produce unique products for each customer, and thereby increase the values achieved from carrying out the activities. Furthermore, in this endeavour the resources and activities of the firms involved in relationships are 'confronted' which enables the firms to find or create new combinations of activities and resources. These new combinations may result in better products in terms of enhancements of their performance, production methods resulting in lower costs and/or better quality, etc.

Building on von Hippel (1988) and Pasinetti (1981), Håkansson (1993: 214) argues that increasing specialisation may be an effect of heterogeneity, i.e., the value of resources is determined by how they are combined, but also a factor increasing the heterogeneity further: 'The specialisation process increases the possibility and the benefits of using external specialists'. This is an effect of the mutual learning firms may achieve through interaction.

The difference between the two ways of organising the set of activities (illustrated in Figure 6.1) can also be described and analysed from the standpoint of the nature of the boundaries around the activities and resources of the firms. In the vertically integrated firm with market exchange on both sides, the firm boundary clearly *separates*, or even isolates (as discussed above), the firm from its environment. In the other structure the firm boundaries do not separate the firms but rather *relate* them to one another. In the first structure, illustrated in Figure 6.1, the possibilities of combining activities and resources are therefore set within the firm's boundary, while in the second structure they are interdependent of other firms' activities and resources.

Adam Smith asserted that the division of labour is limited by the extent of the market, but the extent of the market was also expressed as the 'power of exchange'. Thus, considering the two distinct forms of exchange (i.e., market and relationship), the 'power of exchange' may take on new meaning when relationships are used as a form of co-ordination. The mutual connection between the situational conditions and the co-ordination provided by relationships may be what the 'power of exchange' is about when relationship exchange is applied as a form of co-ordination. The dynamics evolve out of the relationships being both the result *and* cause of the ever changing interdependence among the activities and resources of firms in industrial systems.

In 'real' industrial systems there may be no clear cut examples of the sort illustrated in Figure 6.1, i.e., either exclusively market or relationship exchange around a firm. Most firms rather live with a mixture of co-ordination forms. The presence of relationship exchange in the 'mix' of co-ordination forms may create a dynamic force, while the standardisation required by market exchange may provide a means of dealing with the complexity of the system, since it is not possible to interact with too many counterparts at the same time. Consequently, there is no possibility for the individual firm to utilise all resource heterogeneity, i.e., to exploit all combination possibilities (Håkansson 1993).

RELATIONSHIPS – HOW TO LIVE THEM

Considering the 'living' character of relationships, they cannot be managed since new combinations resulting from 'confrontations' among activities and resources can hardly be planned in advance. However, there may be different ways to *live* in relationships in terms of how the firms involved let 'confrontations' take place. In the SweFork case it was frequently emphasised that the suppliers perceived themselves as becoming involved too late in development projects meaning that the components, or systems, were already specified by SweFork when the suppliers became involved. Hence, SweFork used the suppliers as mere subcontractors. In doing so, SweFork neglected to take advantage of the potential benefits that 'confrontations' among its own and the suppliers' resources and activities could have entailed. The rationale was explained as 'things are too complicated already', and therefore the potential solutions to the technical problems provided by suppliers were not taken advantage of. Rather, the suppliers were assumed to affect the development projects negatively by adding their own concerns, which would only complicate matters further. The results, however, were either that adjustments had to be made when SweFork considered the design complete (which impacted on other components and systems), and/or that inefficient production methods were used, or that poorly designed products were produced. For instance in the steering arm case, SweFork's lack of competence about injection moulded plastic components resulted in extensive design changes when production and sales of the T2–truck had already started, as well as in dissatisfied customers. However, note that individuals at SweFork were concerned about the effects of not involving the suppliers when new products were

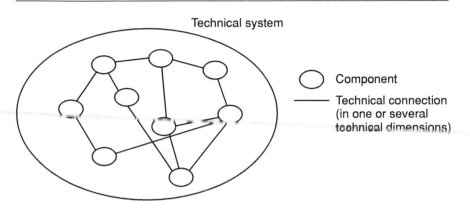

Figure 6.2 SweFork's perception of the general technical system constituting a truck

developed since they were aware of the fact that this behaviour often forced the suppliers to use obsolete production methods.

Contrary to SweFork's perception of interaction making product development more complicated, living in relationships can be seen as a means of dealing with complexity. The way SweFork dealt with the technical system, constituting its trucks, in principle, is illustrated in Figure 6.2.

When new trucks were developed this was mainly done in-house, with the focus on technical interdependence among components within the truck which, hence, defined the technical system of concern. Thereafter suppliers were chosen to produce the already specified components or systems within the truck. At this stage the suppliers were forced to try to adapt its resources to fit the specified component or system. The result was that the technical dependence on the suppliers' resources was predominantly unilateral.

In Figure 6.3, a simple example illustrates the relations between a component and the resources it becomes connected to through the relationship with a supplier. The implications are obvious. Had SweFork let 'confrontations' take place at a stage when mutual adjustments were possible, (a) it would have been possible to capture similarities in the production of the components to a greater extent, and (b) the supplier's knowledge about combining certain resources, e.g., what technical properties feature different combinations such as the strength in certain materials in connection with the physical shapes determined by the tools, could have been utilised to a greater extent.

Furthermore, through 'confrontations' among the resources and activities of the respective firms the knowledge about the effects of combining them increases, which may result in further adjustments impacting on the conditions setting the terms for the proper forms of co-ordination as discussed

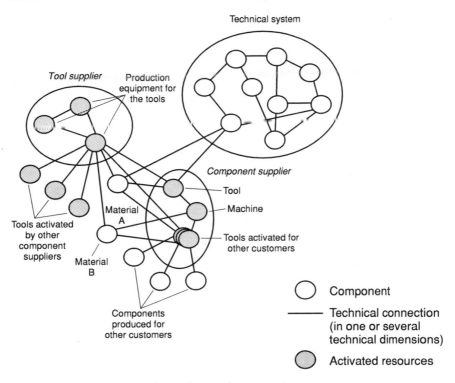

Figure 6.3 Technical interdependence of concern for a component

above. In terms of technical systems, new technical connections and dimensions may be discovered. Obviously, the structural requirements for developing knowledge about the combinations are greater when firms specialise, as shown in Figure 6.3, rather than if SweFork, for instance, had internalised the production of the component as well as of the tool.

Although the example is simplified in terms of the number of connected components and activated resources involved, it illustrates the complexity characterising technical systems. Still, it only concerns one component in a technical system comprising hundreds. The complexity resulting from taking all relevant (in terms of technical interdependence) elements into account is immense. If the various technical dimensions the technical interdependence may appear in are also taken into account, the complexity increases further, and in one way or another this complexity must be dealt with.

Obviously, 'guidelines' cannot be given, but, inspiration may be found. Jung's description of the 'energy of life' and how it results from two opposite dynamic processes may be one source of such inspiration. The variation between these dynamic processes (extroversion and introversion directed externally and internally) according to Jung gives rise to the 'energy of life'. Through extroversion, adjustments to the external environment, referred to as progression, are made. Through introversion adjustments to the 'self' – regression – are made. Hence, concentrating solely on co-ordinating the activities and resources within one's own firm's boundaries means that the 'energy' will be less than if this is combined with 'relating' to counterparts, or, to put it differently, by letting 'confrontations' with the activities and resources of the own firm with those of its counterparts take place. According to the description of how SweFork dealt with the technical development of its truck, regression, i.e., adjustments among components within one's 'own' narrowly defined technical system, dominated, making progression almost impossible since at the stage when suppliers were involved there were only limited possibilities to adjust the components to the suppliers' resources.

In current models dealing with the division of labour, technical development is generally considered to be undertaken *within* firms. Relationships may be used as means to reduce production costs, but this is considered to be at the expense of reduced 'flexibility' in technical development. For instance, Langlois and Robertson (1995: 23) consider interdependence among firms problematic in relation to technical development:

> Because these forms of coordination have been designed, or have evolved, they also add to the element of inflexibility present in the factory system because they may be inapplicable if their stages of production are altered significantly in either a systemic or an autonomous fashion.

According to Langlois and Robertson (1995: 35) dynamic transaction costs can only be overcome by the firm. Dynamic transaction costs are defined in two ways by Langlois and Robertson:

1 the costs of persuading, negotiating, co-ordinating and teaching outside suppliers, and
2 the costs of not having the capabilities you need when you need them.

Here it is argued that relationships not only provide access to capabilities or resources that may be needed at a particular moment (which may not be possible to identify in advance), but that the need itself is probably differently specified as a result from interaction.

How the firm perceives itself as part of a larger context affects its behaviour. If it perceives itself as part of a firm-market context, as described in most models of industrial systems, this entails a certain behaviour, as the firm considers itself independent of individual counterparts. However, if the firm is involved in relationships with specific counterparts, the firm may consider itself integrated in its context owing to a certain awareness of the interdependence among activities and resources across its formal boundaries. In this respect the firm and its perception of itself as part of a wider context resembles the individual's. In Jung's framework the problematic is dealt with using the distinction between the 'I' and the 'self'. While the 'I' is described as the part of ourselves we are aware of (i.e., on the surface), the 'self' lies deeper. We may strive to come closer to the 'self', and this contributes to the development of the individual into a more integrated personality. To understand, or come closer to, the 'self' the connection between the individual and the collective is explored. Jung does this by studying the connection from many perspectives. He considers this necessary since he assumes that nothing concerned with human behaviour has only one meaning. Thus, there is no such thing as simple rational action, but rather there are numerous fragments of reasons embedded in the structures and in the minds of the actors acting within it. The same may be true when it comes to dynamics in highly complex industrial systems.

Bibliography

Alchian, A.A. and Demsetz, H. (1972) 'Production, Information Costs, and Economic Organization', *The American Economic Review* 62: 777–95.

Axelsson, B. and Easton, G. (eds) (1992) *Industrial Networks – A New View of Reality*, London: Routledge.

Babbage, C. (1832) *On the Economy of Machinery and Manufactures*, reprint M. Kelley, NewYork, 1963.

Bångens, L. (1997) 'Industrial Networks, Firms, and Markets: An Exploration of their Role in Capability Accumulation in the Third World, with a Focus on sub-Saharan Africa', dissertation, Department of Industrial Marketing, Chalmers University of Technology (forthcoming).

Bångens, L. and Dubois, A. (1995) 'Network Dynamics as Transitions among Co-ordination Forms', paper presented at the 2nd Workshop on Technological and Industrial Development, Wiks slott, 22–23 November.

Barreyre, P.Y. (1988) 'The Concept of "Impartition" Policies: A Different Approach to Vertical Integration Strategies', *Strategic Management Journal* 9: 507–20.

Blois, K.J. (1971) 'Vertical Quasi-Integration', *Journal of Industrial Economics* 20(3): 253–72.

Boulding, K. (1953) 'Toward a General Theory of Growth', *The Canadian Journal of Economics and Political Science* 19: 326–40.

Carlsson, B. and Jacobsson, S. (1992) 'Technological Systems and Economic Performance: The Diffusion of Factory Automation in Sweden', paper presented at the EARIE Annual Conference, Ferrara, Italy, 1–3 September.

Coase, R.H. (1937) 'The Nature of the Firm', *Economica* 4: 386–405.

Corsi, M. (1991) *Division of Labour, Technical Change and Economic Growth*, Avebury: Aldershot.

Culliton, J. (1942) 'Make-or-Buy', dissertation, Harvard Graduate School of Business Administration, Boston.

Dirrheimer, M. and Hubner, T. (1983) 'Vertical Integration and Performance in the Automotive Industry', paper presented at the Future of the Automobile Forum, Boston: MIT.

Dixon, D.F. and Wilkinson, I.F. (1986) 'Toward a Theory of Channel Strucure', *Research in Marketing* 8: 27–70.

Dubois, A. and Håkansson, H. (1997) 'Relationships as Activity Links', in M. Ebers (ed.) *The Formation of Inter-organizational Networks*, Oxford: Oxford University Press.

Englander, E.J. (1988) 'Technology and Oliver Williamson's Transaction Cost Economics', *Journal of Economic Behaviour and Organization*: 339–53.

Eriksson, A-K. and Åsberg, M. (1994) 'Kostnadseffekter av affärsrelationer – Fallet Gärdin and Persson AB', dissertation, Department of Business Administration, University of Uppsala.

Ford, D.I. (ed.) (1990) *Understanding Business Markets*, San Diego, California: Academic Press.

Ford, D., Cotton, B., Farmer, D., Gross, A. and Wilkinson, I. (1993) 'Make-or-Buy Decisions and their Implications', *Industrial Marketing Management* 22: 207–14.

Gadde, L.-E. and Håkansson, H. (1993) *Professional Purchasing*, London: Routledge.

Håkansson, H. (ed.) (1982) *International Marketing and Purchasing of Industrial Goods. An Interaction Approach*, London: John Wiley.

—— (ed.) (1987) *Industrial Technological Development. A Network Approach*, London: Croom Helm.

—— (1989) *Corporate Technological Behaviour – Cooperation and Networks*, London: Routledge.

—— (1992) 'Networks as a Mechanism to Utilize Heterogeniety', working paper, Department of Business Studies, University of Uppsala.

—— (1993) 'Networks as a Mechanism to Develop Resources', in P. Beije *et al.* (eds) *Networking in Dutch Industries*, Leven-Apeldorn: Garant, 207–22.

—— (1994) 'Economics of Technological Relationships', in O. Granstrand (ed.) *Economics of Technology*: Elsevier Science.

Håkansson, H. and Snehota, I. (1995) *Developing Relationships in Business Networks*, London: Routledge.

Hayes, R.H. and Abernathy, W.J. (1980) 'Managing Our Way to Economic Decline', *Harvard Business Review*, July–August, 67–77.

Hippel, E., von (1988) *The Sources of Innovation*, New York: Oxford University Press.

Jauch, L. and Wilson, H. (1972) 'A Strategic Perspective for Make or Buy Decisions', *Long Range Planning*, 12 December: 56–61.

Johanson, J. (1966) 'Svenskt kvalitetsstål på utländska marknader', dissertation, Department of Business Administration. University of Uppsala.

Johanson, J. and Mattsson, L.-G. (1987) 'Interorganizational Relations in Industrial systems: A Network Approach Compared with the Transaction-Cost Approach', *International Studies of Management and Organization* XVII(1): 34–48.

Jung, C.G. (1995) *Om psykisk energi, drömmar och arketyper*, (A. Leander, (ed.)), Stockholm: Wahlström and Widstrand.

Lamming, R. (1989) 'The Causes and Effects of Structural Change in the European Automotive Components Industry', International Motor Vehicle Program, Center for Technology, Policy and Industrial Development, Cambridge: Massachusetts Institute of Technology.

—— (1993) *Beyond Partnership – Strategies for Innovation and Lean Supply*, New Jersey: Prentice-Hall.

Langlois, R.N. (1989) 'Economic Change and the Boundaries of the Firm, in B. Carlsson (ed.) *Industrial Dynamics*, Lancaster: Kluwer Academic Publishers.

Langlois, R.N. and Robertson, P.L. (1995) *Firms, Markets and Economic Change: A Dynamic Theory of Business Institutions*, London: Routledge.

Leenders, M. and Nollet, J. (1984) 'The Gray Zone in Make or Buy', *Journal of Purchasing and Materials Management*, Fall: 10–15.

Leijonhufvud, A. (1986) 'Capitalism and the Factory System', in R.N. Langlois (ed.) *Economics as a Process: Esays in the New Institutional Economics*, New York: Cambridge University Press: 203–23.

Loasby, B.J. (1991) *Equilibrium and Evolution – An Exploration of Connecting Principles in Economics*, Manchester: Manchester University Press.

Lundgren, A. (1994) *Technological Innovation and Network Evolution*, London: Routledge.

Lundvall, B.-Å. (1988) 'Innovation as an Interactive Process: From User–Producer Interaction to the National System of Innovation', in G. Dosi *et al.* (eds) *Technical Change and Economic Theory*, London: Pinter Publishers: 349–69.

Marshall, A. (1920) *Principles of Economics*, London: Macmillan and Co.

McGuiness, T. (1991) 'Markets and Managerial Hierarchies' in G. Thompson *et al.* (eds) *Markets, Hierarchies and Networks*, London: Sage Publications.

Milgrom, P. and Roberts, J. (1992) *Economics, Organization and Management*, New Jersey: Prentice-Hall International, Inc.

Nooteboom, B. (1993) 'Networks and Transactions: Do they connect?', paper presented at the 9th Conference on Industrial Marketing and Purchasing, Bath, UK.

OECD report (1992) 'Technology and the Economy – The Key Relationships', Chapter 3: Innovation-Related Networks and Technology Policymaking: 67–87.

Panzar, J.C. and Willig, R.D. (1981) 'Economies of Scope', AEA Papers and Proceedings, May: 268–272.

Pasinetti, L. (1981) *Structural Change and Economic Growth – A Theoretical Essay on the Dynamics of the Wealth of Nations*, Cambridge: Cambridge University Press.

Penrose, E.T. (1959) *The Theory of the Growth of the Firm*, Oxford: Basil Blackwell.

Piore, M. (1992) 'Fragments of a Cognitive Theory of Technological Change and Organizational Structure', in N. Nohria and R. Eccles (eds) *Networks and Organizations. Structure, Form and Action*, Boston: Harvard Business School Press.

Richardson, G.B. (1972) 'The Organisation of Industry', *The Economic Journal*, September: 883–96.

—— (1975) 'Adam Smith on Competition and Increasing Returns', in A.S. Skinner and T. Wilson (eds) *Essays on Adam Smith*, Oxford: Clarendon Press.

Richardson, G.B. (1995) 'The Theory of the Market Economy', *Revue Economique*, 6 November: 1487–96.

Smith, A. (1986) *The Wealth of Nations*, Books I–III (with an introduction by Andrew Skinner), London: Penguin Books.

Stigler, G.J. (1951) 'The Division of Labor Is Limited by the Extent of the Market', *The Journal of Political Economy*, 3 June: 185–93.

Stuckey, J. and White, D. (1993) 'When and When Not to Vertically Integrate', *Sloan Management Review*, Spring: 71–83.

Swedberg, R. (1994) 'Markets as Social Structures' in N.J. Smelser and R. Swedberg (eds) *The Handbook of Economic Sociology*, Princeton: Princeton University Press.

Teece, D.J. (1976) *Vertical Integration and Vertical Divestiture in the U.S. Oil Industry: Analysis and Policy Implications*, Stanford: Stanford University Institute for Energy Studies.

—— (1982) 'Towards an Economic Theory of the Multiproduct Firm', *Journal of Economic Behavior and Organization* 3.

Thompsson, G., Frances, J., Levacic, R. and Mitchell, J. (1991) *Markets, Hierarchies and Networks. The Coordination of Social Life*, London: Sage Publications.

Turnbull, P.W. and Valla, J.-P. (eds) (1986) *Strategies for International Industrial Marketing,* London: Croom Helm.

Venkatesan, R. (1992) 'Strategic Sourcing: To Make or not to Make', *Harvard Business Review*, November–December: 98–108.

Walker, G. and Weber, D. (1984) 'A Transaction Cost Approach To Make-or-Buy Decisions', *Administrative Science Quarterly* 29: 373–91.

Waluszewski, A. (1989) 'Framväxten av en ny mekanisk massateknik', dissertation, Department of Business Studies, Uppsala University.

Weick, K.E. (1969) *The Social Psychology of Organization*, Reading: Addison-Wesley.

Williamson, O.E. (1975) *Markets and Hierarchies: Analysis and Antitrust Implications*, New York: Free Press.

—— (1979) 'Transaction-Cost Economics. The Governance of Contractual Relations', *The Journal of Law and Economics* 22: 232–62.

—— (1985) *The Economic Institutions of Capitalism*, New York: The Free Press.

Womack, J., Jones, D. and Roos, D. (1990) *The Machine That Changed the World*, New York: Rawson Associates.

Young, A. (1928) 'Increasing Returns and Economic Progress', *Economic Journal* 33: 527–42.

Index

Abernathy, W.J. 5
activities: closely complementary
23–24, 30–32, 110; complementary
23–24, 30, 110, 120; dissimilar 24,
30, 68; exchange 18, 28–29, 73–74,
106, 111–112; general 54, 87, 103,
109–116; production (*see* activities:
transformation); similar 23, 30–34,
55–59, 64–68, 73–75, 85–86, 89–108,
111–117, 120–122, 126; (customer or
end product) specific 55, 70, 87, 91,
103, 109–116; 'switchboard' for
102–107; systematic closely
complementary 23–24, 30–32;
transaction (*see* activities:
exchange); transformation 18, 27–29,
75–76, 99, 101, 105, 107, 111–113
activity: chains 25–34, 54–57, 65–67,
70–75, 83–89, 93–95, 102–107,
109–119; links 20, 34, 66–67, 86, 91,
105
activity structure 3, 21, 25–36, 54–58,
64–68, 72–75, 83–129; dynamics of
120–129; end product related
(or specific) 26–36, 92–108,
109–119
actor bonds 20
Alchian, A.A. 19
Åsberg, M. 16
asset specificity 12
automotive industry 3, 7, 52
awareness 114–119
Axelsson, B. 15

Babbage, C. 9
Bångens, L. 115, 122
Barreyre, P. Y. 4, 6
Blois, K. J. 15

Boulding, K. 34, 124
boundaries 110–119; awareness 109,
114–116, 118; firm 2, 13, 23–34,
106–108, 111, 118, 124; general-
specific 110–115, 118; influence 109,
118
bounded rationality 11

calculations 6, 43, 44, 59, 60, 80, 91
capability 47, 65, 72, 91, 128; special
23, 30 (*see also* resources)
capacity 81–82, 85, 95; excess 42, 78;
fixed 37, 41, 96; lack of 68, 76, 105;
utilisation 62, 90, 95, 103, 123;
variations 47
Carlsson, B. 16
classical economic theory 7–11
Coase, R.H. 11, 13, 16
combinations (of resources and
activities) 120–127
component (*see* product)
compromises 108, 116
'confrontation' 121–128
connectedness 16, 91
continuity 15
contractual relationships 12–13
control 43–44, 46, 54, 65–67, 81,
116
co-ordination: activity 5, 14, 22–36,
92–119; mode or form 11–14, 17, 21,
23–24, 30–36, 120–128
Corsi, M. 7
cost accounting 6, 43
cost function 22
cost structure 66, 81, 91, 95,
105
Cotton, B. 3–5
Culliton, J. 2, 5